CONTENTS

Introduction *4*

BACKGROUND
Geography *6*
History *8*
People and Culture *15*
Lombardy's Artists 20

EXPLORING THE ITALIAN LAKES
Must See *22*
Milan *24*
Excursions from Milan *34*
Bergamo *37*
Brescia *41*
Verona *44*
The Great Lakes *52*
  Lake Maggiore *52*
  Lake Lugano *59*
  Lake Como *64*
  Lake Garda *72*
The Smaller Lakes *81*
  Lake Idro *81*
  Lake Iseo *81*
  Lake Orta *82*
  Lake Varese *83*
The Lakeside Villas 84
The Trentino *86*
  Lakes of Trentino *89*
  Castles of Trentino *91*

ENJOYING YOUR VISIT
Getting About on the La *94*
Weather *95*
Calendar of Events *96*
Accommodation *97*
Food and Drink *102*
Shopping *106*
Entertainment and Nightlife *108*
Sports *109*

A-Z FACTFINDER
The Basics *112*
A-Z Information *114*

Index *127*

KT-116-952

INTRODUCTION

One of the great railway experiences is to be had on the overnight express from Paris to Milan. Around 7am, the smell of coffee drifts encouragingly from the restaurant car after the long uncomfortable night. The train begins to pick up speed as though shaking off the frontier delays at Basel, the long haul through the Simplon, the first Italian stop at Domodossola. It plunges into a tunnel and there then follows, for the next 15 minutes or so, a series of dramatic snapshots as the train emerges into daylight and then plunges back into darkness. The snapshots could be that of a holiday brochure as the train hurtles along the shore of Lake Maggiore. The colour of the lake is so intense that only the heraldic term 'azure' really fits, while the green of trees and mountains, and the white of clouds and distant snow-covered peaks complete the picture. Click! and there is a shot of yachts skimming like gulls. Click! and poplars frame the view. Click! the distant shore disappears altogether then rushes back. Click! the lake itself disappears as the train enters the Plain.

For 2 000 years, the rich and sensitive have flocked to enjoy the beauty of the Italian lakes, from Catullus, the Roman poet, to Hemingway, the American novelist. The lakes nestle in a world suspended between the last slopes of the Alps and the great Po Plain. Four lakes are world famous: Maggiore, Lugano, Como and Garda, but there are many, many more. Some are hidden like jewels in dense woodland or among remote mountain peaks, accessible only by tracks. Others form the natural

Snow-capped peaks form an Alpine backdrop to the resort of Menaggio on Lake Como.

ITALIAN
LAKES
— in your pocket —

MAIN CONTRIBUTOR: RUSSELL CHAMBERLIN

PHOTOGRAPH CREDITS
Photos supplied by The Travel Library:
Stuart Black back cover, 9, 13, 17, 18, 21, 27, 29, 30, 32,
34, 35, 36, 39, 40, 42(t,b), 43, 46, 47, 48, 51, 61, 63(t,b),
66, 67, 68, 76, 77(t,b), 79, 82, 83, 85(t), 87, 89, 90, 92,
100, 116, 121, 123, 125; Alan Copson 50; Andrew Cowin
5, 6, 65, 69; Philip Enticknap front cover, 23, 24, 53, 54,
55, 56, 85(b), 94, 103, 106, 124; Greg Balfour Evans 62,
80, 119; Mike Kipling 74; Derek Organ 8, 108, 111; David
Robertson title page, 71, 72, 97, 113; Alex Stephen 33,
58; Mark Stone 31; David Young 15
Other Photos:
Pinacoteca di Brera, Milan/Bridgeman Art Library,
London 12, 20; Accademia Carrara, Bergamo/Bridgeman
Art Library, London 38.

*Front cover: view over rooftops, Stresa, Lake Maggiore; back
cover: Milan Cathedral; title page: decorated pot of geraniums.*

MANUFACTURE FRANÇAISE DES PNEUMATIQUES MICHELIN

Place des Carmes-Déchaux – 63000 Clermont-Ferrand (France)

© Michelin et Cie. Propriétaires-Éditeurs 1998

Dépôt légal Avril 98 – ISBN 2-06-652101-9 – ISSN 1272-1689

No part of this publication may be reproduced in any form

without the prior permission of the publisher.

Printed in Spain 3-98

MICHELIN TYRE PLC
Tourism Department
The Edward Hyde Building
38 Clarendon Road
WATFORD Herts WD1 1SX - UK
☎ (01923) 415000

MICHELIN TRAVEL PUBLICATIONS
Editorial Department
One Parkway South
GREENVILLE, SC 29615
☎ 1-800 423-0485

highway for bustling communities. Scattered among them are enchanting small towns, villages and castles, and to the south, within easy reach, are some of the great historic cities of Italy. The great lakes are intimately linked to the cities of the Plain. Como is only 30 minutes by train from Milan, one of the largest cities of Europe; a motorway runs a mile or so from the southern borders of Garda. But they retain their inviolability.

GEOGRAPHY

In good weather conditions – a fine winter's morning is ideal – looking north from the foothills of the Apennines it is just possible to see the towering ice wall of the Alps. This mighty chain of mountains has shaped Italian history. The vast plain between Apennines and Alps is something of an anomaly. Northerners regard it as part of Italy but it has always been a little apart from the Italian Peninsula.

Winding its way through the plain is Italy's longest river, the Po, which empties itself in a confusion of mouths in the Adriatic. It is navigable to large boats inland as far as Pavia, some 38km (24 miles) south of Milan. Historically important, medieval merchants used it to bring goods from the other side of the world right into the heart of Italy. Architects used it as a cheap and safe means of transporting the mountains of stone required to build the cities, while soldiers used it to carry warfare to other areas.

Filling the deep channel gouged out by vast glaciers, the fiord-like Lake Como is surrounded by steep mountains.

Other major rivers run from the north. The mightiest of these is the Adige, running down from the high mountains at a great pace through its own valley in the east of the region. When man eventually arrived in the area he was grateful for the natural highway carved by the river and today the modern main road faithfully follows it. The Mincio drains Lake Garda to the south, while the Ticino from Lake Maggiore joins the Po at Pavia, with the lush green plain stretching between them.

Made fertile by the alluvial deposits from these rivers draining from the Alps, the Po Plain (or Lombardy Plain) is one of the richest agricultural areas in Italy and, perhaps, Europe, growing everything from rice and grapes to maize and vegetables. During the Ice Age, the same forces which created the lakes also added to this richness. Vast glaciers moving south ground out the moraine which was deposited over the plain.

As the glaciers gouged out their paths, they left behind vast cavities, which after the Ice Age filled with water to form the lakes. The deepest of these is Como, at some 410m (1 345ft). The southern lakes tend to narrow, their sides growing steeper, to the north. These towering sides, coupled with temperature variations, create different wind effects happily exploited by modern yachtsmen. Como, for example, has two different wind patterns – the *tivano*, blowing north to south in the morning, and the *breva*, blowing in the reverse direction later in the day.

HISTORY

The northern frontier of Italy presents a textbook example of the pressures which have created the nations of Europe. Four nation states border this frontier: France, Switzerland, Austria and what used to be

A reconstruction of a Bronze Age 'house on stilts', at Lake Ledro.

known as Yugoslavia. Over the centuries, they endlessly contended for power and land, sometimes through outright war, sometimes through marriage, and sometimes through diplomatic trading. Early rock inscriptions indicate that the Po Plain was inhabited by **early man** from about 3 000 BC, followed by settlers during the **Bronze Age**.

Influence of the Romans

The northern part of Italy has always been apart from the Italian Peninsula; in the 7C BC, when most of Italy was populated by the **Italics**, the region was invaded from the north by the **Celts**. The **Gauls** dominated the region until the **Romans** moved

The Capitoline Temple, in Brescia, was built by Emperor Vespasian in AD 73. It was covered by a mudslide in medieval times which helped preserve the ruins.

northwards in the 3C BC into the land they called 'Cisalpine Gaul', Gaul this side of the Alps. Over the next few centuries the Romans gradually overcame opposition from the Celtic tribes, establishing a strategically important province, with Mediolanum (Milan) as its capital, from which campaigns to expand the empire could be launched.

Under the Romans, the northern regions developed into a prosperous area, with thriving towns at Verona, Genoa, Turin, Brescia, Bergamo and Como. By the 5C AD, however, the decline of the Roman Empire meant that the area was unable to withstand the **Visigoth** invasion.

The Arrival of the Lombards

Successive waves of **barbarians** arrived to plunder the rich lands of northern Italy. Some, like the Huns, simply departed with their loot but others, like the Ostrogoths, created stable governments.

The last to arrive, in AD 568, were heavily bearded men, probably from Scandinavia, whom the native Italians called 'Longobardi' (long beards). They became known as **Lombards**, and were to give their name to most of the great plain between the Alps and the Apennines which they soon dominated. They established their capital in Pavia until 774, when the greatest of all northern kings, Charlemagne, arrived and added Lombardy to his domains which he ruled from Aachen (Aix-la-Chapelle), in Germany. Crowned Emperor of the West on Christmas Day 800, Charlemagne brought back stability to Italy but his Carolingian Empire barely survived his death in 814.

Guelphs and Ghibellines

Chaos returned to Italy, with the cities forming themselves into sovereign city-states. In theory, they belonged to one of two factions: the **Guelphs**, who owed allegiance to the Pope, and the **Ghibellines**, who supported the Emperor. In practice, however, these allegiances were simply party labels, to be used as politically convenient; for example, the Ghibelline city of Milan led a rebellion against the Emperor Frederick Barbarossa in 1176, while the Guelph city of Florence did not hesitate to attack the Pope's representatives in a long-drawn-out war in the 14C. In Lombardy, most cities fell under a 'despot', usually the most ruthless and efficient member of a ruling family.

The feudal cities continued to fight among themselves until, by the 15C, only Venice and Milan remained independent, with all the other Lombard cities controlled by one or the other. Venice was content simply to protect her possessions on the mainland, but Milan embarked on an ambitious programme of empire-building until she controlled cities deep in Tuscany and high in the Alps. The **Visconti** family not only secured Milan's position as the richest and most powerful city in Italy, but through marriage within the royal families of England and France established influential European connections.

Foreign Influences

Unfortunately, Milan was tied into a dynastic web which would bring tragedy to all Italy. The French King Charles VIII was asked by Ludovico il Moro to intervene, and in 1494 invaded Italy at the head of an immense army, triggering off a series of foreign

Ludovico il Moro (1452-1508) is depicted in typical fashion, with his family kneeling before Madonna and Child. This great Sforza ruler revived the Court of Milan.

invasions. The Emperor Charles V also claimed the city through his Habsburg inheritance, and the two great powers fought out their differences, at the expense of the Italians. Emperor Charles prevailed, but that merely added one more twist to Milan's fate, for in 1712 the Austrian Habsburgs staked their claim. The French briefly re-appeared in the late 18C when Napoleon invaded and had himself crowned 'King of Italy', but after his overthrow in 1815 the Austrians returned, brutally suppressing the nascent Italian nationalism.

The legendary Giuseppe Garibaldi, who played an important role in bringing about the unification of Italy.

Towards Unification

However, the desire for independence was growing among Italians in the north, resentful of Austrian rule. In Piedmont a strong nationalist group was developing around the figure of Vittorio Emmanuele II of Turin, supported by such charismatic figures as Mazzini, Cavour and Garibaldi. (Every Italian city today will have a main street, usually a 'Corso', named after one of these patriots.) On 24 June 1859, two tremendous battles just south of Lake Garda smashed the power of Austria. The first was at San Martino della Battaglia, where Vittorio Emmanuele destroyed the main body of the Austrians. A tower on the site of the battle, open to the public, commemorates the occasion. On the same day, at Solferino a few miles south, Vittorio Emmanuele's ally, Napoleon III, vanquished the remnants of the army. It was at the **Battle of Solferino** that the Swiss J H Dunant was so horrified by the suffering of the wounded that he later proposed the founding of what would become the International Red Cross.

In 1861 Vittorio Emmanuele was crowned King of Italy. In 1865 he moved his court to Florence and finally, in 1870, entered Rome and so established a unified Italy.

The World Wars

Less than a generation later, however, Northern Italy again became a battlefield when the **First World War** broke out. One of the bloodiest battles of the war took place at Caporetto, in October 1917, when half a million Italians died fighting the Austrians. The **Fascist movement** saw its origins in Milan after the war, with the Fascists coming to power in 1922.

Despite the loss of life during the First World War, the region as a whole suffered far more in the **Second World War**, particularly after the Italians joined the Allied side in 1943 and the Germans dug in for their last line of defence. One of the many architectural losses was the beautiful Ponte Scaligero at Verona, blown up along with many other bridges to impede the Allied advance. Ironically it was around Lake Garda, one of Europe's most favoured playgrounds, that there took place the last act of the Fascist tragedy which had scarred Italy for a quarter of a century. In 1944, on the direct order of Adolf Hitler, **Benito Mussolini**, the Italian dictator who had been deposed and imprisoned, was rescued and established in the puppet government, the Italian Social Republic, at Salò on the west bank of the lake. In April 1945, while trying to retreat northwards to the relative safety of Germany, Mussolini was captured at Dongo on Lake Como and shot, his body taken to Milan and exposed to public humiliation.

Post-war Recovery

Post-war, Lombardy shared in Italy's astonishing economic recovery. So prosperous has it become that there are complaints that it is 'carrying' the backward South and demands have been made that it should secede and form its own independent republic, the League of the North. It seems unlikely that Italy will abandon the unity for which it fought so long and hard, but the desire for secession is a reminder of the strong sense of locality that underlies all Italian thinking to this day.

PEOPLE AND CULTURE

Regionalism lies at the very heart of Italian society. Language, cuisine, architecture and customs are all linked directly to locality. As far as Italians are concerned, there is no such person as an 'Italian'. There are Tuscans and Umbrians and Calabrians. There are Milanese, Veronese, Pisans. A Veronese may not always understand a Neapolitan, while a Neapolitan is as unfamiliar with the Milanese cuisine as any foreigner. Lombardy shows this trait to an extreme degree, for here North meets

The traditional way of life continues in many villages.

South, Latin meets Teuton. Fair-haired people are almost as common as dark.

Yet binding them all together is their awareness of *italianità* – of belonging to a common 2 000-year-old culture underpinned by a single language, supported by a great religion whose seat is Rome. Indeed, religion infuses everyday life in an unselfconscious, almost casual, way. The festival of the local patron saint is an important social occasion, and one of the few things to give offence to this otherwise tolerant people is indecorous dress or behaviour in a church.

Italians may differ from region to region, but they share one great characteristic: interest in, and hospitality to, the foreigner, despite having been swamped by visitors for century after century. They are content to take their holidays in their own beautiful, infinitely variegated country but are still endlessly curious about others. They are not great linguists – outside the obvious tourist centres it is as well to know some basic Italian phrases – yet they make up for it by enthusiastically welcoming even the most halting attempts to speak Italian.

Commedia dell'arte

A fashion in late-Renaissance Italy was for groups of travelling actors, usually about a dozen, who would travel the country, stopping off at towns to give dramatic performances. The plays, written by the group and accompanied by music, might be tragedies, pastorals or comedies, but the latter were most popular with the large crowds they attracted. The stock characters would enact scenes between the lords and their servants, who provided comic relief in the form of slapstick. Between acts the crowd would be amused by displays of juggling, dance and magic by the players. Although cultured Italians despised the performances, in a repressed country *commedia dell'arte* provided an outlet for people to express their opinions, for example through the character of Arlecchino (or Harlequin), thought to have been been the creation of an actor born in a small village north of Bergamo.

Music

The region has long been associated with music and, in particular, opera, with Milan's world famous La Scala and Verona boasting the prestigious Arena. **Gaetano Donizetti** (1797-1848), born in Bergamo, wrote charming comic operas such as *L'Elisir d'Amore* and *Don Pasquale* in addition to melodramas like *Lucia di Lammermoor*. Perhaps the greatest composer of the time, **Verdi** (1813-1901) chose Milan as his home, producing the dramatic works for which he is so well known – *Nabucco, Rigoletto, Il Trovatore, La Traviata, Aida* and, of course, his *Requiem*. **Rossini** (1782-1868) and **Bellini** (1801-1835) performed at La Scala, whose great conductor, **Arturo Toscanini** (1867-1957), was renowned for the vitality and originality of his performances.

Gaetano Donizetti seeks inspiration for his next opera in the gardens of his home town, Bergamo.

Architecture

The Italian Lakes area, like the rest of Italy, is blessed with a wealth of art and architectural gems, from the **Neolithic** period to modern art of the 20C. Early **rock carvings** can be seen in the valleys north of Lake Iseo, notably Valle Camonica. There are few reminders of the Celts' and Ligurians' settlements, but the **Romans** left several magnificent monuments, notably Brescia's forum, Verona's wealth of Roman ruins, including the Arena, and villas on the shore of Lake Garda, at Sirmione and Desenzano.

Architecturally, there were three great waves of building in the region, followed by an odd postscript or codicil in the 17C and 18C, when the wealthy built splendid villas on the shores of the lakes. The first period was the **Romanesque** – which Italians rather confusingly call 'Romanico'. This was the fusion of classical Roman models with northern ideas. An important example of the Lombard-Romanesque style is the church of Sant'Ambrogio in Milan, founded in the 4C and enlarged in the 9C and 11C. It was to be the model for other great churches and cathedrals in the region, such as

The Basilica of Sant'Ambrogio in Milan was to become the prototype of Lombard-Romanesque cathedrals in the region.

Cremona, Lodi and Monza. The architects deliberately took the Roman basilica, or law court, as a model. A basilica was a rectangular building with an apse, or curved recess, at one end in which the judge sat. The Christians took the same idea but placed an altar in the apse. The idea of the basilica was developed further in Verona with the magnificent church of San Zeno Maggiore, the most ornate in Northern Italy, with its façade of marble tiles.

A genuine home-grown talent were the **Maestri Comacini** (master-builders) of Como. They originated as early as the 7C, and specialised in stone-cutting and the use of coloured marbles. The Maestri Comacini were at their peak in the 12C and 13C, and eventually examples of their work spread throughout Europe and even as far as Russia.

The next architectural development in Lombardy, though only short-lived, was born of the tremendous flowering of church architecture in France in the 13C. As this trend moved south, there was again a fusion of ideas and **Italian Gothic** was born. The supreme example is the great cathedral of Milan, begun c1386.

The 14C and 15C saw the influence of Florence's great **Renaissance** architecture and art. By this time, each of the cities (except Venice) was under the control of one immensely wealthy family. Its members, anxious to show both their power and taste, were able to attract talented artists and architects to their courts. The most famous of these was Leonardo da Vinci, who accepted the invitation of the Sforza Duke of Milan. Unfortunately, little that he created there has survived.

Lombardy's Artists

The great wealth of the local families enabled them to patronise talented artists from the south. Nevertheless, Lombardy produced a number of painters who in any other country but Italy would have been hailed as being of the first rank, but tend to be over-shadowed by their southern rivals, particularly from Tuscany.

Pisanello (c1395-c1450), from Verona, was the greatest exponent of the Veronese School, who developed a Gothic art form which combined flowing lines with a meticulous attention to detail. **Bernardino Luini** (c1481-1532) was born in the village of Luino, on Lake Maggiore, and owed much of his fame to following the style of Leonardo da Vinci. He remained and worked in and around Milan, where the Brera Gallery displays much of his work, though perhaps his greatest achievement is the fresco in Santa Maria degli Angioli, in Lugano. **Ambrogio Bergognone** (1460-1523) was another home-grown artist content to stay at home, most of his work being in the Certosa of Pavia.

Madonna and Child with St Anne, by Bernardino Luini (Brera Gallery, Milan).

An art form highly characteristic of the area, in particular of the Trentino, is that of the **mural**. Such wall paintings, many of great size and complexity and occurring both inside and outside, are usually executed in fresco. The artist must not only be highly skilled but able to work at great speed, for the painting is done on wet plaster which dries rapidly (fresco = fresh). The mural then becomes part of the plaster and, when dry, will last as long as the plaster lasts, usually for centuries, sometimes for millennia.

Frescoes (c1460) in the Sforza Castle, Milan.

MUST SEE

Arena**, Verona

Completed around AD 30, this enormous building probably held the entire Roman population of Verona, and can still accommodate some 25 000 spectators in 44 tiers of the original stone seats. It is the venue for an important festival of music and opera each July and August – book early to ensure your place at one of the magical performances in this world famous amphitheatre.

Isole Borromee***
(Borromean Islands),
Lake Maggiore

These three beautiful little islands would justify a visit to the lake for themselves alone. They are named after the noble Borromeo family, the local family who produced San Carlo Borromeo. In the early 17C Count Carlo Borromeo transformed the barren rock of **Isola Bella*** (Beautiful Island) into superb gardens, set out on ten terraces descending to the lake. Crowning the island is the Borromeo palace, open to the public. **Isola Madre*** (Mother Island), is largely covered by a famous botanical garden, and **Isola dei Pescatori**, as its name implies, is occupied by fishermen.

Duomo*** (Cathedral), Milan

Begun in 1386 under the direct orders of Gian Galeazzo Visconti, building has gone on almost to today: the last of the five bronze doors was erected as recently as 1965. The Cathedral is, nevertheless, Italy's supreme example of Gothic architecture, with its gables, pinnacles, statues and belfries of gleaming white marble. Napoleon had himself crowned 'King of Italy' in the Cathedral in 1805.

Certosa di Pavia***
(Charterhouse of Pavia)

In a country of outstanding architecture the Certosa is widely recognised as being one of the most outstanding examples of Lombard architecture, with its intricate pattern of coloured marbles on the façade and the magnificent murals and paintings inside. Founded in 1396 as the mausoleum for the Visconti family of Milan, its tombs include those of Gian Galeazzo Visconti, the first duke of Milan, and Lodovico Sforza and his wife.

Grotte di Catullo**
(Grotto of Catullus), Sirmione

The Roman poet Catullus (87-54 BC) built himself a splendid villa, whose ruins today form an important archaeological site. Unlike many such sites, it is set pleasantly among trees, creating an attractive green oasis at the tip of the peninsula.

Monte Mottarone★★★

A mountain vista of a kind usually obtained only by hours of strenuous climbing can be accessed by the mountain road. Mottarone is 1 491m (nearly 4 500ft) high and presents a tremendous view of the Alps and seven of the lakes to east and west, and the Po Plain to the south. In good weather, it is even possible to see the pinnacles of Milan Cathedral.

Villa Carlotta★★★, Tremezzo

This is perhaps the most opulent of the splendid villas on Lake Como, now owned and maintained by a Trust. Originally built in Baroque style, with neo-Classical additions in the early 19C, its superbly restored rooms contain a wealth of sculptures and paintings. The world-famous gardens, with their mixture of Italian and English landscape design, are a pure delight, offering lovely views across Lake Como.

The terraced gardens of Isola Bella, on Lake Maggiore, were designed to resemble a ship.

MILAN★★★

The Latin name for Milan – Mediolanum or 'mid-land' – exactly describes both its position and the reason for its importance. It stands in the centre of the great Plain of Lombardy, linking north to south, east to west. Before the development of air transport it was the gateway to Italy, for to the north are the Alpine passes, and to the south the great Roman road, the Via Emilia, providing access through the Apennines. Today, as Italy's second city, Milan is a hub of rail, air, road and, until recently, even water transport. So important was the railway that the Stazione Centrale, begun in 1912 and taking 21 years to complete, is now a historic monument in its own right. A million and a half people live in the municipal region and

Trams trundle through the busy streets of Milan.

some four million in Greater Milan. It is to Rome what New York is to Washington – brash, thrusting, go-ahead, the commercial, industrial and fashion capital of Italy. Indeed, for over 100 years between AD 286 and 402, when Rome was sunk in barbarism and the emperor resident in Constantinople, Milan was the capital of the Western Roman Empire.

During the medieval period when every Italian city was a sovereign state, Milan was the first to fall under the rule of a single family, the Visconti, in the 14C. The Visconti expanded their power throughout almost all of the Plain of Lombardy, coming into contact with the expanding powers of Venice in the east and Florence in the south. In 1395 Gian Galeazzo Visconti purchased the title of 'duke' from the Western Emperor

Map of Milan
- **C** *Palazzo dei Giureconsulti*
- **D** *Palazzo della Ragione*
- **M¹** *Museo del Duomo*
- **M⁷** *Casa del Manzoni*
- **T²** *Conservatorio*

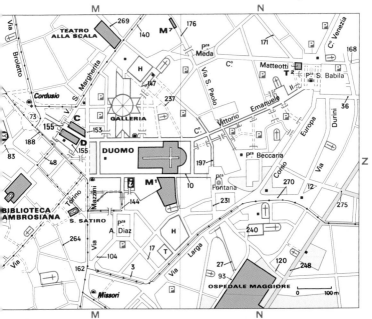

Wenceslas, so creating the first of the Italian dukedoms, and might well have brought about the unification of Northern Italy had he not died suddenly of the plague in 1402. The *condottièro* (mercenary soldier) Giovanni Sforza usurped power and there followed the long-drawn-out struggle first between France and Spain, and then between France and Austria, for the possession of Italy. During these conflicts Milan changed hands several times, finally achieving freedom from the Austrians after the Battle of Magenta in 1859.

The city played a leading role in the **Risorgimento** – the movement for the unification of Italy – and in 1919 Benito Mussolini founded the Fascist Party there.

The Milanese vigorously adopted new technology after the First World War, developing now world-famous industries such as Pirelli, Isotta Fraschini and Alfa Romeo. (The car company still uses the arms of the Visconti, a serpent swallowing a man, as its logo.) Money poured into the city. Fashion followed suit – nowhere else in Italy can you better see illustrated the Italian phrase *bella figura* (cutting a dash) than in the shops and streets of Milan. You need a deep purse and a considerable amount of time fully to appreciate Milan, but behind the glittering, towering office blocks and modern factories is a city rich in history.

The city was heavily bombed during the Second World War, La Scala Theatre and the Castello Sforzesco being particularly badly damaged. The Italian tradition of preferring to restore rather than rebuild means that the wartime scars are no longer visible, although there have been some regrettable post-war developments. Despite the size of the modern city, most of the historic monuments can be visited on foot. A good point of departure is the Piazza del Duomo, almost at the centre of the medieval town. There are more than 50 museums and galleries in Milan, in addition to significant historic buildings and private galleries. What follows is a selection of the most important.

Duomo*** (Cathedral)

Although the city has vastly outgrown its medieval origins, the magnificent Gothic cathedral is still at the very heart of Milan. Building began in 1386, under Gian Galeazzo Visconti, and continued throughout the 15C and 16C, using the greatest builders of the time. The façade was completed in 1809 under the orders of

The stunning beauty of Milan's Gothic Cathedral is best appreciated in the golden light of late afternoon.

Napoleon. It is the biggest church in Italy,
apart from St Peter's in Rome, and its
statistics are impressive. It can hold 25 000
people standing; there are 2 245 statues on
the **exterior***, culminating in a forest of
some 135 pinnacles, the highest reaching
108m (354ft). It is possible to ascend to the
roof, either by steps (nearly 200 of them) or
by lift, for a breathtaking **walk*** with
panoramic views.

The **interior*** is less elaborate than the
exterior with its gleaming white marble and
exquisite statuary, but its imposing size and
the stunning stained glass windows, with
their glorious colours and flamboyant
Gothic tracery, cannot fail to impress.
To the south of the Cathedral is the **Museo
del Duomo**** (Cathedral Museum),
containing sculptures, tapestries and the
Aribert Crucifix*. It is housed in the **Palazzo
Reale** (Royal Palace), built in the 18C by
Piermarini.

Castello Sforzesco*** (Sforza Castle)

The castle was founded by the Visconti in
the late 14C but largely rebuilt in
Renaissance style by the Sforzas (1451-1466).
Today, it houses the city's art collections in
the **Civiche Collezioni d'Arte** (Municipal Art
Collections), whose 26 rooms cover every
period from Roman to Renaissance. The
sculptures** include the enormous
medieval **tomb of Bernabò Visconti****, with
his looming figure on horseback, and the
unfinished **Rondanini Pietà****, by
Michelangelo. The **Picture Gallery***
contains works by Bellini, Mantegna, Filippo
Lippi and Bergognone, while the collection
of string and wind instruments in the
Museum of Musical Instruments* includes a

spinet played by Mozart.

Apart from the castle, another attraction here is the **Parco Sempione** (Sempione Park), one of the two major green areas in the city centre. The park, very popular at weekends and holidays, contains the **City Aquarium** and the **Arco della Pace**. Napoleon intended this as his triumphal arch, based on the Arch of Severus in Rome, but after the Battle of Waterloo it was hurriedly transformed into the Arch of Peace.

The Sforza Castle houses some of Milan's greatest works of art, including this massive 14C tomb of Bernabò Visconti.

The courtyard of the Brera Palace, which houses the extensive collection of the Brera Picture Gallery.

Pinacoteca di Brera★★★
(Brera Picture Gallery)

Begun in 1651, the first floor of the Palazzo di Brera houses the Pinacoteca, the most important collection of North Italian painting. Among the major works represented are **The Dead Christ★★★** by Mantegna, Giovanni Bellini's *Pietà* and **Marriage of the Virgin Mary★★★** by Raphael. As with so many Italian monuments, it has been under restoration for some years and certain rooms may be closed.

Teatro alla Scala★★ (La Scala Theatre)

Another 'first' for Milan – the world's most famous opera house. It owes its name to the church of **Santa Maria della Scala** (St Mary of the Staircase) on the site of which it was built from 1776 to 1778. Some of Italy's greatest composers made their national début here, including Verdi, Rossini and Bellini, and the composer Toscanini placed it on the international stage. The **Scala Museum★**, a theatrical museum, is attached.

Museo Nazionale della Scienza e Tecnica Leonardo da Vinci★
(Leonardo da Vinci National Museum of Science and Technology)

As its name implies, pride of place is given to Leonardo's technological inventions. Other sections include astronomy, acoustics and telecommunications, with large pavilions displaying means of transport. The building was a 16C convent, restored after war damage.

Museo Poldi-Pezzoli★★
(Poldi-Pezzoli Museum)

On the Via Manzoni, which runs in front of La Scala, is the lovely 17C palace of Gian Giacomo Poldi-Pezzoli, which houses an important collection of paintings, weapons, **clocks★** and bronzes. Pride of place among the paintings goes to Piero del Pollaiolo's 15C **Portrait of a Woman★★★**, but there are numerous other wonderful works to look out for, like **Madonna and Child★★** by Botticelli, and Giovanni Bellini's **Dead Christ★**.

The plain exterior of the world-famous La Scala belies the magnificence of its auditorium.

Museo Bagatti Valsecchi★★
(Bagatti Valsecchi Museum)

Two brothers, Fausto and Giuseppe Bagatti
Valsecchi, built a neo-Renaissance palace in
which they could integrate their collection
of fireplaces, friezes and ceilings.

Sant'Ambrogio★★ (Basilica of St Ambrose)

The oldest church in Milan and one of the
most important in Lombardy, this Lombard-
Romanesque basilica was begun in 379 and
consecrated by St Ambrose himself. It was
enlarged in the 9C and 11C, and again in
1150 when the magnificent **atrium★** was
added. The interior is rich in Byzantine-style
marbles and **mosaics★**.

*The Byzantine
influence on this
5C mosaic in
Sant'Ambrogio is
apparent, it is
thought to be a
portrait of St
Ambrose himself.*

Santa Maria delle Grazie★
(Church of St Mary of Grace)

Visitors tend to overlook this gem of a
church, largely completed by Bramante in
1492-1499, in favour of the modest
monastery refectory attached to it where,

high on an interior wall, is Leonardo da Vinci's **Last Supper★★★** (1497). Endlessly experimenting, he used oil paint instead of tempera on the plaster and the work began to deteriorate in his own lifetime. Despite major attempts at restoration (the last in 1976), deterioration continues and it is only a matter of time before it disappears completely. But Leonardo's majestic concept is still clear: the blessing Christ, St Peter with his forefinger indignantly upraised, and Judas scowling on the left.

Giuseppe Mengoni, designer of Milan's elegant shopping arcade, Galleria Vittorio Emanuele, accidentally fell to his death from the roof just before its opening.

Galleria Vittorio Emanuele★
(Vittorio Emanuele Gallery)
Begun in 1865 to the design of Giuseppe

Mengoni, Italy's most famous – and expensive – shopping arcade was completed in 1878. It takes the form of a four-armed star, with one arm connecting the Duomo to La Scala, and along its length are luxurious cafés, restaurants and shops where the Milanese mingle with the tourists.

EXCURSIONS FROM MILAN

An excellent railway system and a good road network make it easy to get away from Milan for a day.

Abbazia di Chiaravalle★
(Chiaravalle Abbey)

7km (4 miles) south-east of Milan centre. Accessible by tram as well as train. By road, leave the city by Porta Romana.

Founded by St Bernard of Clairvaux in 1135, this is the largest Cistercian abbey in Italy. Although altered in the 17C, the interior is still French Gothic. Of special note is the polygonal **bell tower★**.

Chiaravalle Abbey represents one of the earliest examples of Gothic architecture in Italy.

Monza

21km (13 miles) north-east of Milan, on the S 36.
Today best known for its international motor
racing, Monza has a history which goes back
beyond Milan's. The racing circuit is in the
northern part of the vast landscaped **Parco
di Villa Reale★★** (Park of the Royal Palace).

In the town, enclosed in the altar of the
13C **Duomo★** is the **Iron Crown of Monza★★**,
reputed to contain a True Nail of Christ's
Cross. All Holy Roman Emperors were
crowned with it after 1311, and Napoleon
used it for his 'coronation' in Milan
cathedral.

Pavia★

*38km (24 miles) south of Milan, on the S 35
(turn left for Certosa di Pavia before reaching
Pavia). Or take the A 7 south for 19km (12 miles)
and then left onto the S 526 to Pavia.*
The favourite summer retreat of the Visconti
of Milan (the **Castello Visconteo★** is now a
museum★), Pavia is still a delightful riverside

*The impressive
Castello Visconteo
was built in 1360
for Gian Galeazzo,
the great Visconti
ruler.*

town, rich in Romanesque remains. It is a refreshing place in which to relax and unwind after the hectic pace of Milan.

The famous **Ponte Coperto** (Covered Bridge), built in 1354 on Roman foundations, was weakened by bombs and collapsed in 1947. It was rebuilt to a different design.

About 8km (5 miles) north of the city is the **Certosa di Pavia★★★** (Charterhouse). Founded in 1396 as the mausoleum for the Visconti family of Milan, it was built in the 15C and 16C. A major feature of the **façade★★★** is the use of coloured marbles to form intricate designs. The **interior★★★** is rich in paintings and murals: look for the mural of a Carthusian monk gazing pensively into the nave. There are two important tombs: that of Gian Galeazzo

Considered to be the greatest example of Renaissance architecture in Lombardy, the elaborate façade of the Certosa di Pavia.

Visconti, the first duke of Milan who founded the Certosa, and that of Ludovico Sforza (Il Moro) and his wife Isabella. Carthusians lived in separate cells, each with its own garden, and these form another complex attached to the church. It is a favourite spot for Sunday visitors from Milan. On sale is the famous liqueur, Chartreuse, made to a secret recipe by Carthusian monks, and a special cosmetic cream, also produced by the monks, made out of beeswax.

BERGAMO★★ AND BRESCIA★

These two cities could be called non-identical twins, quite different in appearance but sharing important characteristics. Each is a great city in its own right: Brescia with a population of 200 000 inhabitants is second in Lombardy only to Milan, while Bergamo is not far behind, with over 130 000. Each is situated on the foothills of the Alps, with its feet on the Plain and its head in the hills. Each is the key or gateway to valleys leading deep into the mountains and to the lakes. And although each has now far outgrown its medieval core, that core has been jealously preserved, so there is much to see.

BERGAMO★★
The city is an outstanding example of the Italian skill of town building, the ability to graft the old onto the new so that both benefit. There are, in fact, two Bergamos: Città Bassa (Lower Bergamo) on the Plain, mostly the creation of this century, and the historic Città Alta (Higher Bergamo), set on a hill.

CITTÀ BASSA★ (Lower Town)

Set in an area of attractive alleyways is the
Accademia Carrara★★ (Carrara Academy).
This is one of Lombardy's major art
galleries, founded in the 18C by Count
Giacomo Carrara. It has a particularly fine
collection of works by Venetian artists,
including Giovanni Bellini's *Madonna and
Child* (compare it with his father Jacopo's
painting of the same subject), Vittore
Carpaccio's *Six Saints* and Titian's *Orpheus
and Euridice.* There is also a remarkable
work, *Calvary*, by the German Albrecht
Dürer.

*Madonna and Child
by Giovanni Bellini
(Carrara Academy,
Bergamo).*

The railway station and all the major
hotels and shops are in the Lower Town,
which is bisected by one of those rather
fearsome avenues called *viali*, of which the
Italians are fond. This is named after two
Italian heroes, Vittorio Emmanuele II, and
the best-loved pope of this century, Giovanni
XXIII, who died in 1963. He was born
Angelo Roncalli in a village in the Province
of Bergamo. Leading off the *viale* is **Piazza
Matteotti★** with the **Teatro Donizetti**
(Donizetti Theatre) named after the
composer who was born in Bergamo in
1797. At the end of the *viale* a modern
funicular will take you up into the Upper
Town and another world.

CITTÀ ALTA★★★ (Upper Town)

This is the picturesque, older part of the
town which contains some of the finest
buildings. One of the delights of the Upper
Town is the sudden glimpses of the world
outside – the great Plain to the south, the
towering mountains to the north – seen
from its castle and streets. It is a place for
casual wandering, for every piazza and street

is of interest, but the following attractions should not be missed. The first four are located around the attractive **Piazza del Duomo★★**, and the arcades of the Palazzo della Ragione in the north lead to the **Piazza Vecchia★**, the heart of the old town.

Santa Maria Maggiore★

Built in the 12C, this is one of the most important Romanesque churches in Lombardy. Altered many times over the centuries, the interior is mostly Baroque and is a treasure house of art, including 16C Florentine **tapestries★★** and a monument to Donizetti.

Cappella Colleoni★★ (Colleoni Chapel)

This beautiful Renaissance chapel was built against the wall of Santa Maria Maggiore as a mausoleum for Bartolomeo Colleoni. Born in Bergamo (1400), he became a famous *condottiero* (mercenary soldier) who captained both the Venetian and Milanese

The domes and towers rise up over the rooftops of the Città Alta, Bergamo.

armies. The face on his splendid equestrian monument differs markedly from the fierce, eagle-like face on Verrochio's great statue of him in Venice. Nearby is the exquisite tomb of Colleoni's daughter, Medea.

Duomo (Cathedral)

On the other side of the Colleoni Chapel is Bergamo's cathedral. The building of the present cathedral extended over a period of 400 years. Begun in the mid 15C, it was not completed until the 19C when the west front was added. Opposite stands the octagonal Battistero* (Baptistery), built originally in 1340 as part of the church of Santa Maria Maggiore and rebuilt here in 1898.

The ornate Colleoni Chapel contains the two-tiered tomb of Colleoni and his wife, topped with a golden equestrian statue.

Piazza Vecchia★

This is the heart of Bergamo, with its beautiful fountain and the 16C **Palazzo della Ragione** (Palace of Justice). High on the front of the palazzo is the Winged Lion of San Marco – a reminder that Bergamo was the westernmost town held by the Venetian Republic, the last bastion against Milan. The Lion is modern, the original having been destroyed in a revolt in the 18C.

Rocca (Fortress)

Both the Visconti of Milan and the Venetians had a hand in building this castle in the 14C. It provides magnificent **views★** of the old town and countryside.

BRESCIA★

The city, seat of the last king of the Lombards in the 8C, has played a leading role in Lombardy ever since it was founded by the Romans. It felt the full force of the Barbarian invasions from the north: Lombards, Ostrogoths, Byzantines, Venetians, French and Austrians have each ruled it in turn.

Brescia was heavily bombed during the Second World War but the damage has been skilfully repaired, and there are fine examples of architecture from the Roman, Renaissance and Baroque periods, overlooked by the medieval castle.

Duomo (Cathedral)

Instead of demolishing the old to make way for the new, the Brescians built their **Duomo Nuovo** (New Cathedral), begun in 1604, beside the **Duomo Vecchio★** (Old Cathedral). The latter, known as the Rotonda because of its circular shape, dates from the early 12C and was built on the Roman baths.

Broletto
To the left of the New Cathedral, this was originally Brescia's city hall, built around 1200 and now used as the Prefettura (police headquarters). Soaring over it is the Torre del Popolo, nearly a century older.

Tempio Capitolino★
(Capitoline Temple)
The picturesque **Via dei Musei★** leads to the heart of Roman Brixia. The **Tempio Capitolino★** was built by the Emperor Vespasian in AD 73 and, its fragments brilliantly restored, it now houses the **Civico Museo Romano★** (Museum of Roman Antiquities). The most famous exhibit is the superb Winged Victory, a bronze statue nearly 2m (6ft) tall. Near the Temple are the unexcavated remains of the Roman theatre.

Brescia's Duomo Nuovo and Duomo Vecchio sit side-by-side.

Detail of Roman carvings from the Capitoline Temple, Brescia.

Castello
This massive building has witnessed every period of Brescia's turbulent history, for although the main body of the castle dates from the 14C it is built on a Roman fort. It contains the **Luigi Marzoli Museum**, with displays of 14C-18C weaponry. The granary houses the **Museum of the Risorgimento** and the castle stands in an attractive park.

Loggia★
This beautiful Renaissance building, begun in 1492, was partly designed by the great Venetian architects Sansovino and Palladio.

The Clock Tower in the Piazza della Loggia echoes the great clock tower in St Mark's Square, Venice.

Numerous artists contributed to the sculptured details, which include heads of the Roman emperors. It replaced the Broletto as the city hall.

Pinacoteca Tosio-Martinengo★
(Tosio Martinengo Art Gallery)
Lombard artists, in particular those of the Brescian school, are well represented in this, the city's major art gallery. They include Moretto's (1498-1554) *Christ and the Angel*, and various portraits by his pupil, Giovanni Moroni (1520-1578).

Monastero di San Salvatore e Santa Giulia★
Built in the 9C by Byzantine architects from Ravenna, the **Basilica of San Salvatore** uses much material from Roman buildings from the site, including the columns of the nave. The 16C church of **Santa Giulia★** contains interesting treasures from the Lombard period, including the **Cross of Desiderius★★**.

VERONA★★★

In the delightful little Piazza delle Erbe
of Verona stands an elegant stone pillar,
crowned with the figure of a winged lion.
Today it is a much loved and cherished
monument, but when it was erected it was a
symbol of dominance. The Winged Lion was
the emblem of St Mark, patron saint of
Venice, and the column was erected to
symbolise and emphasise the Venetian
conquest, in 1405, of a once independent
city.

For year after year and century after
century, from the fall of the Roman Empire
until the unification of Italy in 1870, these
beautiful cities of Italy were always at war
with each other, pausing only to fight off
foreign invaders – Spanish, Austrian and
French – who sought to add the jewel of Italy
to their crowns. And when there were no
outside enemies, the citizens turned on each
other in feuds between rival families.
Shakespeare's tragedy of *Romeo and Juliet* is
based on a real situation, even if the people
are fictitious; families tore and savaged each
other in real life, as the Montagues and
Capulets did in drama.

Most major Italian cities are Roman in
origin but, apart from Rome itself, few show
their ancestry so clearly as does Verona. A
Roman bridge still crosses the deep, rushing
torrent of the Adige, leading to a Roman
amphitheatre on the far side; a Roman
triumphal arch marks the entrance to the
city; and, above all, there is the enormous
Arena – the third largest amphitheatre in
the Roman world and better preserved even
than the Colosseum in Rome.

After the fall of the Empire, Verona went
through the usual savage internecine

Map of Verona

M¹ *Archaeological Museum*

B *Palazzo Maffei*

D *Palazzo della Ragione*

E *Loggia del Consiglio*

P *Palazzo della Governo*

J⁷ *Palazzo dei Tribunali*

fighting until one family, the **Scaliger**, emerged as dominant. Italians love to bestow nicknames, and the nicknames given to the Scaliger attest their ferocity: Mastino (Mastiff), was followed by Cangrande (Big Dog) while the last Scaliger was Cansignorio (Lord Dog). But the Veronese were also cultured, giving shelter to Dante from 1301-1304 during his exile, and under Cangrande I, Dante's host, Verona achieved cultural heights. The family ruled Verona for over a

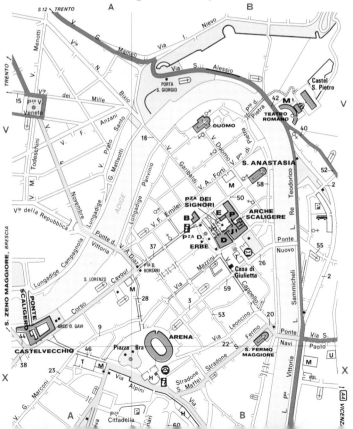

century, until the city fell to the Visconti of Milan in 1387. They were expelled in turn by the Venetians. Venice ruled for 400 years until the Napoleonic conquest of 1796.

The city, with a population of around 250 000, most of whom live outside the historic centre, is easy to get round on foot. The Adige winds its way in a great curving 'S' through the city, crossed by nine bridges and with the heart of the city tucked away on a kind of peninsula. There are two main centres: that based on the great open space,

View of the historic city of Verona from Castel San Pietro overlooking the Roman Ponte di Pietra with the Duomo in the background.

Piazza Bra, with the Arena as the backdrop, and the intimate little streets and squares around **Piazza delle Erbe★★**. The site of the original Roman forum, Piazza delle Erbe is an enchanting, friendly spot, with its fountain crowned by the statue known as the Madonna of Verona, its fruit and vegetable stalls and its restaurants and cafés.

Piazza dei Signori★★

This piazza was the original centre of government, almost entirely enclosed with an entrance through a monumental arch from the Piazza delle Erbe. On the right is the **Palazzo della Ragione** (Palace of Justice), the medieval seat of government, built around 1193, with the **Torre dei Lamberti** (Lamberti Tower), built in 1464. You can reach the lantern of the tower by lift or stairs for a splendid view of the city.

Joined to the Ragione by another arch is the sinister **Palazzo dei Tribunali** (Palace of

A statue of Dante, father of the Italian language who took refuge in Verona during his years of exile, stands pensively in the Piazza dei Signori.

the Tribunals) with boxes for denunciations. Dante lived in the Scaliger **Palazzo del Governo** in 1303, and there is a statue of him in the centre of the piazza, erected in 1865.

Arche Scaligere★★ (Scaliger Tombs)

These are probably the most extraordinary medieval funerary monuments in Italy, and an excellent example of Gothic Veronese art in the 13C and 14C. Dominant is the monument to Cangrande I (d. 1329), made of pink Verona marble and crowned with an equestrian statue of the prince grinning in a most curious manner (a copy of the original is in Castelvecchio). Tombs of other rulers, from Mastino (d. 1277) to Cansignorio (d. 1375), are behind a wrought-iron grille against the Romanesque church of **Santa Maria Antica**. The ladder motif which features on the coat of arms on the sarcophagi is a pun on the name Della Scala (of the steps), the true family name of the Scaligers.

Casa di Giulietta (Juliet's House)

Also in this area is Juliet's House. Such is the power of Shakespeare that, not only is there no justification for associating Juliet with this 13C house in Via Cappello, but Juliet herself never existed outside a 16C *novella*. The house does, however, have a balcony and is now firmly on the tourist circuit, with lovers plighting their troth in the form of graffiti on the courtyard walls. (*Open to the public.*)

Sant'Anastasia★

Close by is Verona's largest church, begun in 1290 and completed in the 15C. The vast interior was designed to hold the huge

Lovers from all over the world come to Juliet's balcony to pledge their love.

congregations who came to listen to the sermons of the Dominicans. In addition to its important works of art, look for the supporters of the holy-water stoups, in the form of life-like hunchbacks known as *Gobbi*.

Duomo★ (Cathedral)

Set at the end of the peninsula bounded by the Adige is the Duomo. Verona's wealth of Romanesque and Gothic churches rather steal the thunder of the Cathedral. Not least of its interest is the way it bridges the centuries, combining both Romanesque elements below and Gothic above. In the first chapel of the north aisle is the *Assumption* by Titian. The Cortile Sant'Elena is a pure Romanesque cloister.

Ponte di Pietra (Stone Bridge)

Close to the Duomo is the original Roman bridge, at the bend of the river. On the far side is the **Teatro Romano★** (Roman Theatre), even older than the Arena but discovered only in the 19C and heavily restored. Adjoining it is the **Museo Archaeologico** (Archaeological Museum). The **Castel San Pietro**, higher up the hill, provides an excellent panoramic **view★★** of the city across the river.

Giardini Giusti (Giusti Gardens)

Tucked away behind No 2 Via Giusti is this enchanting garden, laid out in the late 16C and combining formal and natural elements. Open to the public, it provides a refreshing tranquil spot in the city centre.

Arena★★

Completed around AD 30, this enormous building probably held the entire Roman

The spacious Piazza Bra has as its backdrop the impressive Roman Arena.

population of Verona, and originally measured 150m (492ft) long and 125m (410ft) wide. After the ravages of time and the force of several earthquakes, it is slightly smaller, but no less impressive. Its Italian name, 'arena', is significant for it was used primarily not as a theatre but for bloody combats between gladiators, between men and animals and, latterly, for the martyrdom of Christians. Today it is used for immensely popular operatic and theatre performances (*July and August*), which attract international artists and audiences.

Ponte Scaligero and Castelvecchio★★
(Scaliger Bridge and Old Castle)
The bridge, with its swallowtail battlements, was built by Cangrande Scaliger II between 1354 and 1375 as an integral part of the castle. The bridge was blown up by the Germans during their retreat in 1945 but has been carefully reconstructed. The castle discharged a military role until 1925, when it was turned into the **Museum of Art★★**. The castle building is well worth exploring in its own right, as well as housing important 12C

The Scaliger Bridge spans the Adige, leading to the Old Castle, built in 1354 by Cangrande Scaliger II.

to 16C works by northern Italian artists, including paintings by Verona's own artist, Paolo Veronese, and works by the Venetian Bellini family.

Arco dei Gavi (Arch of the Gavi)
The original Roman road (now Corso Cavour) led through this triumphal arch, erected in the 1C. Destroyed by the French in 1805, it was re-assembled and moved to this site, next to the Castelvecchio, in 1933.

San Zeno Maggiore★★
Built between 1120-1225, and therefore not so venerable as Milan's Sant'Ambrogio, San Zeno rivals it in importance as an example of Lombard-Romanesque. The columns of the richly decorated porch characteristically rest on couched lions, now almost worn smooth, guarding the bronze **doors★★★**. The crypt is the burial place of a galaxy of saints and bishops, including St Zeno, St Cosmas and St Damian. The church contains an amazing number of 12C to 14C frescoes, notably the fine **triptych★★** of *Madonna and Child* by Mantegna (1459) on the altar.

51

THE GREAT LAKES

The mild climate and beautiful locations have led to the development of the lakes' shores over centuries. Happily, the topography has prevented contiguous development but the shores are studded with villages and towns. Only the most important or interesting are listed here but there are countless other gems awaiting discovery by the curious traveller.
(S) indicates localities in Switzerland.

LAGO MAGGIORE★★★
(LAKE MAGGIORE)

This is the second-largest lake in Italy, some 64km (40 miles) long, 4.8km (3 miles) wide with a maximum depth – just off the village of Ghiffa – of 372m (1 220ft). The Romans called it Verbanus after the verbena which grows so prolifically along its shores. The northern end of the lake is in Switzerland, the more interesting western shore is in Piedmont, and the eastern in Lombardy. Starting at Stresa, the towns round the lake are described in a clockwise direction.
(A main road circumnavigates the entire lake. The lower part of the western shore is served by mainline trains from Milan, the eastern shore by a circuitous route via Varese.)

Stresa★★

Stresa is the most popular resort on the lake and the point of departure for the Borromean Islands. Beautiful in its own right, Stresa attracts artists and writers, as well as tourists. It is a starting point for pleasant walks in the nearby hills, and offers both summer lakeside attractions and winter ski facilities. The historic part of the town is

The lovely Borromean Islands punctuate the blue waters of Lake Maggiore, seen from Monte Mottarone.

centered on **Piazza Cadorna**, but over the years luxurious hotels, villas and gardens have developed. Near the church is the **Villa Ducale** where the philosopher Antonio Rosmini lived and died. There is a scenic toll road from Alpino which leads to the summit of **Monte Mottarone★★★** (1 491m/4 892ft), providing spectacular **views**, weather permitting (in very hot weather, a thick haze reduces visibility considerably).

Isole Borromee★★★ (Borromean Islands)

Named after the noble family, the Borromeo, who had great influence in the

region and still own much property, including two of the islands, **Isola Madre★★★** (Mother Island) and **Isola Bella★★★** (Beautiful Island).

The beautiful island of **Isola Bella★★★**, much admired by writers and poets over the centuries, was in fact man-made. Count Borromeo ordered the fabulous Baroque gardens, populated by white peacocks, and terraces of perfumed tropical plants to be created on what was once just a barren rock. The whole design is devised to resemble a ship. A palace was added in the 17C, also in Lombard-Baroque style, with numerous lavish state rooms. There are also curious 'cave' rooms or grottoes, which offered residents a cool retreat during the heat of the summer.

Isola Madre★★★, the largest island, boasts a splendid tropical garden of rare and exotic plants. The 16C palace contains a ceramics

Intricate knot gardens, terraces and statuary fill the ornate Baroque gardens on Isola Bella.

The quaint and picturesque Isola dei Pescatori.

collection and a display of 19C puppet theatres and marionettes. **Isola dei Pescatori★★** has retained much of its charm, with pretty narrow streets in the fishing village, though expensive restaurants are beginning to change the ambience.

Baveno★

A lakeside resort of Roman foundation, Baveno is quieter than its better-known neighbour, Stresa. There are some delightful old buildings arranged around a charming central square. The view of the Borromean Islands from the promenade is particularly fine.

Verbania

The town is an artificial construction, created in 1939 when the towns of **Intra**, **Pallanza★★** and **Suna** were combined into one commune. It is the nearest thing to a conurbation on the lake, but it is still attractive with its magnolias and historic buildings. The name is a revival of the old Roman name for the lake. Pallanza is a beautiful resort, noted for its wonderful scented flowers, its scenic **quays★★** and its

lake views. **Villa Taranto**★★ has lovely
English-style landscaped gardens.

The pretty resort of Pallanza is noted for its mild winter climate, fragrant flowers and attractive quays.

Cannobio★

The most northerly Italian town on the lake,
Cannobio has Roman origins, with
considerable 12C and 13C remains and an
attractive harbour. In the **Santuario della
Madonna della Pietà** is an allegedly miracle-
working *Pieta*. Just 3km (2 miles) from the
town is the dramatic **Orrido di Sant'Anna**★,
where the Cannobino river crashes through
a gorge.

Locarno★★ (S)

In 1925, leading European statesmen met in
this resort and signed the Treaty of Locarno,
designed to prevent all future wars in
Europe. The town is the capital of the Swiss

Canton of Ticino, which extends deep into Italy. Situated in a beautiful bay at the head of the lake, and backed by mountains, it is an elegant and sophisticated holiday resort with a famous casino and many restaurants. Its 15C **castle** is now a museum. A combination of cable-car and chair-lift will take you to the crest of **Cimetta Cardada**★★ which, at 1 671m (5 482ft), has splendid **views**★. The 15C church of **Madonna del Sasso**★, near the cable-car terminus, has an important work of art, the *Flight into Egypt*, by the Milanese painter Bramantino (1465-1536).

Luino

This relatively large town is a sizeable tourist resort on the Lombard side of the lake. The railway station with its custom house reflects the political complexity of the region, for it is where the Italian line from Milan meets the Swiss line from Bellinzona, and it is necessary to change trains. The town is the birthplace of the Milanese painter, Luini, follower of Leonardo da Vinci. It provides a good base for hikers, with many marked walks and superb countryside dotted with unspoilt villages.

Reno

A beautiful little village in itself, tucked between two headlands, Reno is chiefly famous for the extraordinary 15C Carmelite convent, **Santa Caterina del Sasso** (of the Rock). Set on a ledge on Sasso Ballaro, the church, as its name implies, appears to have grown out of the living rock. According to legend a wealthy merchant, saved from drowning by St Catherine of Alexandria, spent the remainder of his life as a hermit

on the ledge. Closed for many years after a fall of stone, it has been re-opened. Access is via a steep descent of steps but lake steamers also visit it.

Laveno-Mombello
An important lakeside port, famous for its ceramics, Laveno-Mombello is also the terminal of a ferry across the lake to Intra, Verbania's business quarter. In 1859 it was the site of bitter fighting between Garibaldi's soldiers and the Austrians who held the castle on the headland. A funicular leads up to **Sasso del Ferro★★** (1 062m/3 484ft), which provides panoramic views over the Lakes.

Angera★
Originally a Roman military foundation and then developed in the 8C by the Lombards, the delightful little town is dominated by the **Rocca Borromeo**, a splendid fortified palace

Those with a head for heights should take the funicular up to Sasso del Ferro, for spectacular views over Lake Maggiore.

built by the Visconti in 1350 on the site of the Lombard fort, and subsequently embellished by the Borromeo. It is well worth a visit, if only for the **Sala di Giustizia** (Room of Justice) and **Sala degli Affreschi** (Room of the Frescoes), both decorated with 14C **frescoes★★**. Those in the Sala di Giustizia include rare depictions of the exploits of the Visconti. The castle also houses the **Museo della Bambola★** (Doll Museum).

Arona

Although an ancient town (the Palace of the Podestà or Governor dates from the 15C), Arona is both the southern terminus of the lake steamers and an important railway junction, and this has stimulated considerable modern development. It was an important seat of the Borromeo family, who had great influence after the decline of the Visconti. The family's most famous member is San Carlo Borromeo, born in 1538, who owed his rapid promotion (cardinal by the age of 22) to the fact that his uncle was pope. As archbishop of Milan, he gained a reputation for saintliness. The vast **statue★** outside the town, known as the **San Carlone**, was erected in 1679 by a descendant, who was also archbishop of Milan.

LAGO DI LUGANO★★
(LAKE LUGANO)

This is the smallest of the four major lakes and decidedly the most confusing politically. A broad tongue of Swiss territory reaches deep down into Italy, stretching towards Como in the east. The tongue crosses the lake, dividing it into three parts: Italian in the north and south-east, and Swiss in the middle. Travelling around the lake, one is obliged to cross and recross the frontier. At one point indeed, it curls back on itself to create the extraordinary enclave, **Campione d'Italia★**, Italian but on Swiss territory. In character, the lake is wilder and more remote than the other three, with relatively fewer developments around its shore. With its steep, fjord-like shores, the lake enjoys a mild climate, enhancing its appeal to visitors.

Starting from Lugano, the towns are described in a clockwise direction round the Lake. (*The A 9 from Milan goes to Lugano, via Como, crossing the lake at Bissone before heading north through the Alps. Smaller roads run round some of the Lake's shores. Porto Ceresion, on the south-western side, is the terminal for the train from Varese, while mainline trains from Milan and Como go to Lugano via Chiasso. Local trains link Lugano with western towns as far as Ponte Tresa. Steamers link all the lakeside towns, and buses from Como connect Lugano and Campione d'Italia.*)

Lugano★★★ (S)

The major town on the lake is in Switzerland, beautifully situated in a deep bay and flanked by Monte Brè and Monte San Salvatore. With a population of less than 40 000, it is much smaller than Como but has the same air of elegant sophistication. Ironically, it is the best place to see the work of the Milanese artist, Bernardino Luini. The church of **Santa Maria degli Angioli** has three of the finest **frescoes★★**, the most impressive representing a *Passion*. The connection is that Lugano belonged to Milan until it was captured by the Swiss in

The Sighignola, the 'Balcony of Italy' provides far-reaching views of Lake Lugano, the town of Lugano and the surrounding mountains.

1512. The Swiss, however, made recompense of a sort when they allowed Mazzini to set up his headquarters there between 1848-1866, during the Italian struggle against Austrian domination.

Although Swiss, Lugano is overwhelmingly Italian in feel. Its heart is **Piazza della Riforma**, while the façade of the 14C **Cathedral of San Lorenzo** is in the Lombard-Venetian style. The **Riva**, or waterfront, is particularly attractive, having a series of quays with splendid views. The **Villa Ciani**, in the **Parco Civico** (Civic Park), houses an art collection which includes the statue known

A tour boat prepares to leave Lugano for a cruise around the lake.

as *La Desolazione*, a mourning woman supposed to represent Italy under a foreign heel. On the waterfront outside the town, on the east, is another museum in the **Villa Favorita★** which housed an important collection of Italian works of art, assembled by the late Baron Thyssen-Bornemisza. The Italian Old Masters are now on loan to museums in Madrid and Barcelona, but the Villa Favorita still retains European and American modern art collections.

Porlezza

This is the northernmost town on the lake, set in Italy at the junction of three mountain roads, one of which connects it to Menaggio, on Lake Como. The town – little more than a village – is attractive, but the scenery is harsh with a massive mountain range dominating the northern shore.

Detail of a sculpture in the Civic Museum, Campione d'Italia.

Campione d'Italia★

Although politically Italian, the town uses Swiss currency and postal services in an impressive example of international co-operation. It also exploits its curious position by becoming in effect one large casino, and gaming now forms a major source of local income. However, the town boasts a number of handsome historical buildings, for it was the seat of the medieval guild of builders, known as the **Maestri Campionesi**. The **Oratory of San Pietro** (1326) was built by them, as was the chapel of the **Madonna dei Ghirli**, which contains some fine frescoes of the early 15C.

Porto Ceresio

The terminus of the railway from Varese and a point of departure for lake steamers, Porto Ceresio stands in a deep bay with views across to the 'pearl of the lake', Morcote. Travelling north-east you cross the Swiss frontier.

The church of Madonna del Sasso in Morcote has beautiful 16C frescoes, typical of the region.

Ponte Tresa (Tresa Bridge)

Confusingly, there are two towns of the same name, the larger in Italy, the smaller across the River Tresa in Switzerland. The river connects the lake with Lake Maggiore and forms part of the Swiss-Italian frontier.

Morcote★★

The town stands on the tip of a peninsula on one of the most picturesque **sites★★** on the lake. The church of **Madonna del Sasso** (Our Lady of the Rock) has magnificent 16C **frescoes**. Immediately beyond the town is **Monte Arbostora** (826m/2 710ft), and further to the north is **Melide**, at the point where road and rail cross the lake to **Bissone** and the main road south.

LAGO DI COMO★★★ (LAKE COMO)

Como is the most popular of the lakes and the only one with a major city, Como, actually on its shores. It is in the shape of an inverted 'Y' with the eastern arm bearing a different name, **Lago di Lecco**, and having the town of Lecco at its southernmost end. The northern end of Lake Como has been compared to a Norwegian fjord because of its relative narrowness and the mountains rising steeply on each side. Most of the development has taken place along the western shore, the eastern being precipitous for much of its length.

Starting from Como, the towns are described in a clockwise direction round the Lake. *(From Milan the FS (national) train service to Como's main San Giovanni station takes 40 minutes. The slower regional Milano-Nord service runs to Como-Lago station, at the lakeside. Como has rail connections with Lugano and Lecco, while buses run to most towns round*

A magical moment as the last sunlight at dusk catches the mountain sides around Lake Como.

the lake. Car ferries operate between Bellagio, Menaggio, Varenna and Cadenabbia, though some services do not operate between October and March. There are frequent hydrofoil, steamer and boat services connecting the main towns on the lake, and motor boats can be hired from Como.)

Como*

With a population of nearly 85 000, this is a major city in its own right. It produced the skilled masons, builders and sculptors, the **Maestri Comacini**, who from the 7C developed the Lombard style throughout the region and Italy, reaching as far as Russia. It is also a manufacturing city, which

has specialised in the production of silk since the early 15C. But the beauty of its position makes it an extremely popular tourist destination. The main square, **Piazza Cavour**, actually opens onto the lake so that passengers from the lake steamers can step directly into the town centre. Green, sheltering hills rise up on each side, while the great Lombard Plain begins behind it to the south, with Milan within easy distance.

Como has always been of strategic importance, at the head of a natural highway that leads deep into the Alps and beyond. The city centre has retained the street plan of the Roman *castrum* from which it developed, and its circuit of walls is still intact. The citizens played an active role in the *Risorgimento* and welcomed Garibaldi as their liberator in May 1859.

Broletto★★

Built in 1215 as the town hall, the two right-hand arches of this beautiful building were demolished to make space for the cathedral, to which it is now attached. In contrast to its elegant façade of alternate bands of grey, white and red marble is the rough stonework of the Campanile.

Piazza Cavour in Como, with its pavement cafés, hotels and boat landing steps, adjoins the lake on one side.

The vaulted Cathedral ceiling is decorated with distinctive blue and gold embellishments.

Duomo★★ (Cathedral)

Begun in 1396, the building of the cathedral went on for over 400 years, spanning the transition from Gothic to Renaissance. The richly decorated late-Gothic façade, built between 1455 and 1486, has Renaissance statues of the two Roman scholars, Pliny the Elder and Pliny the Younger, who were both born in the city. Inside, the lions supporting the holy water stoup are 12C and come from the church of Santa Maria Maggiore, demolished to make way for the cathedral. The dark **interior★** also reveals numerous paintings by Lombard artists, including some by the Milanese artist, Bernardino Luini (*Adoration of the Magi*, and **Virgin and Child with Saints★**), and two by Gaudenzio Ferrari (1471-1546), who worked in Milan and was influenced by Leonardo da Vinci. Look out also for the magnificent 16C-17C Tuscan and Flemish **tapestries★**.

Museo Civico (Civic Museum)

The Civic Museum is housed in two

adjoining palaces, both worth a visit.
Palazzo Giovio contains an eclectic
archaeological and art collection,
including Roman, Egyptian and
Assyrian antiquities, while **Palazzo
Olginati** is devoted to Giuseppe
Garibaldi.

Piazza San Fedele

This irregularly-shaped, cobbled
square is the historic heart of the city.
The **Basilica of San Fedele★** is believed
to stand on the site of a temple to
Jupiter. Built between the mid 11C
and early 12C, it is an outstanding
example of the work of the Maestri
Comacini. The entrance to the apse
(best viewed from Via Vittorio Emmanuele)
has outstanding Romanesque bas-reliefs.

*Built in 1557,
Cernobbio's
magnificent Villa
d'Este is now a
stunning hotel,
strictly for those
with very deep
pockets.*

Tempio Voltiano (Voltaic Temple)

The physicist Alessandro Volta was born in
Como in 1745, and this classic rotunda in
the Giardini Publici contains his scientific
instruments.

Other Towns Around Lake Como

Cernobbio★★

Cernobbio is the third-largest town on the
lake. It has sufficient industry to give it a life
of its own, but also boasts tourist attractions
such as a charming little harbour and beach.
The oldest part of the town is by the harbour.
The dominant building is the immense 16C
Villa d'Este, now a luxury hotel.

Argegno

This is a pleasant little village with a clear
stream, the Telo, burbling through it and

crossed by a Roman bridge. The river valley makes a pleasant excursion by bus, which goes on to **Belvedere di Lanzo**, with a panoramic view of Lake Lugano.

Tremezzo★★★

This has linked up with **Cadenabbia★★** to form a virtually continuous holiday resort where most of the villas have been turned into hotels. The 18C **Villa Carlotta★★**, with its magnificent garden, is open to the public. The exterior of the villa, begun in the early 18C, is relatively austere; the interior, embellished between 1795 and 1856, has been superbly restored. On display are numerous *objets d'art*, including many from the ex-royal palace in Milan. Of special note are the sculptures, which include a copy of Antonio Canova's *Cupid and Psyche*. The **gardens** combine the best in Italian and English landscape design and are rightly world-famous.

Villa Carlotta, in Tremezzo, was built as a wedding present for Princess Carlotta of the Netherlands.

Menaggio★★

Menaggio is an up-market and chic resort, with its lido, golf course and a welcome cool summer breeze. Behind it are attractive and relatively easy walks in the hills and the road providing access to Italian Lake Lugano, only 12km (7.5 miles) distant.

Gravedona

In the Middle Ages, Gravedona, with its neighbours **Dongo** in the south and **Sorico** in the north, formed the independent 'Republic of the Three Parishes' – an excellent example of the political fragmentation of medieval Italy. It was at Dongo that Benito Mussolini was arrested by Italian partisans in April 1945, while trying to escape to Germany. Gravedona, the most northerly town on the lake, is the most important of the three, with a splendid villa, **Palazzo Gallio**, built in 1586, and a 12C Romanesque church, **Santa Maria del Tiglio★**.

Bellano

Situated at the mouth of the Pioverna river, Bellano combines industry with considerable tourist attractions. The Lombard-Gothic **church** is 14C. A little way inland is a dramatic gorge gouged out by the river.

Varenna★

The pretty town makes a good base for touring, and it is well worth exploring the steep, narrow alleys. The Lombard queen, Theodolinda, is reputed to have built the **Castello Vezio** to the south of the town in the 7C. There is a **Museo Ornitologico** (Ornithological Museum) and the beautiful **gardens★★** of the 16C **Villa Monastero**, just outside the town, are open to the public.

Mandello

The largest town on the eastern shore, Mandello is backed by the towering **Grigna mountains** (2 410m/7 907ft). The church of **San Lorenzo**, though built in the 9C, stands on the site of an even older church.

Lecco

Dramatically situated between two lakes and

on the edge of a national park, Lecco is the second-largest town on Como. The southernmost bridge, **Ponte Azzone Visconti**, was built by the Visconti in 1336. The novelist Alessandro Manzoni was born here in 1785, and his villa is now a museum commemorating him. Although the town of Lecco is somewhat spoilt by industrial developments, the lakes and mountains in the surrounding countryside are some of the most scenic, and offer interesting excursions.

Bellagio★★★

Magnificently perched on the very tip of the peninsula, between Lake Lecco and the southern branch of Lake Como, the town provides a number of outstanding views. Northwards, the foothills of the Alps rise above the dark blue waters of the lake. Immediately across the lake is the beautiful little town of **Tremezzo★★★** (*see* p.69) and a

The town of Bellagio enjoys a splendid position on a peninsula between Lake Lecco (on the right) and Lake Como.

short scramble will take you to the crest of the peninsula, with views across to the east. Behind a façade that resembles a miniature Venice, the town is a delightful maze of little alleys and lanes. Take time to explore the lovely **gardens★★** of **Villa Melzi** and **Villa Serbelloni**.

Isola Comacina, first inhabited by the Romans, derived great wealth from its olive trees, and was nicknamed 'city of gold'.

Isola Comacina (Comacina Island)

The only island in the lake, it was just far enough from the shore to provide an asylum for political refugees during the Middle Ages. It is well worth a visit for its haunting ruins, including those of nine churches. A ferry runs from **Sala Comacina**.

LAGO DI GARDA★★★
(LAKE GARDA)

The largest of all the lakes in Italy, Lake Garda is the most oriented to tourism. The glacier which gouged it out carried the moraine far to the south, extending the lake

**Map of
Lake Garda
and Lake Iseo**
(see p.81)

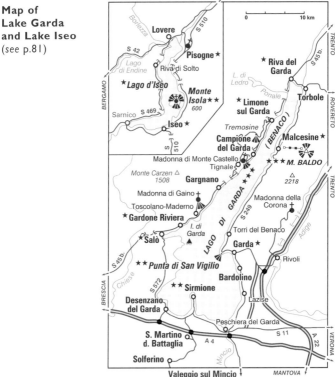

into the Lombard Plain. The rich soil and
mild climate have encouraged both wildlife
and a rich flora. Cedars, olives, lemon trees,
palms, prickly pear and many subtropical
species flourish, and the lake is particularly
rich in fish. The shoreline of most of the
southern half of Garda is flat and this has
encouraged tourist development, in
particular the growth of camping sites.

The **Scaliger of Verona** were the local
ruling dynasty in the Middle Ages and their

castles are dotted around the lake.

The towns are described in a clockwise direction from Desenzano del Garda. (*There are train stations at the southern end of the lake, at Desenzano and Peschiera, where you can also board the hydrofoils and steamers. There are bus services from Brescia, Trento and Verona, and frequent buses from Sirmione to Desenzano and Peschiera. The car ferry operates between Maderno and Torri. The boat and hydrofoil services are reduced between October and March. Timetables are available from the tourist offices. The autostrade from the Brenner encourages*

Monte Baldo, reached by cable-car, provides magnificent views over Lake Garda with the Massifs of Brenta and Adamello to the north,

tourism from the north, from Germany in particular, while the autostrade connecting Brescia and Verona in the south brings in both Italian and foreign tourists from the two big cities.)

Desenzano del Garda

The presence of a railway station makes this pretty little lakeside town a particularly popular holiday resort, for it is only a little over half an hour by rail from the major city of Brescia. It is also a major departure point for lake steamers. Ruins of a Roman villa, **Villa Romana**, have been uncovered, with **mosaics★** dating from the 4C, and there are other Roman remains including part of the foundations of a basilica.

Salò★

This was the seat of the short-lived puppet 'Republic of Salò', established by Benito Mussolini after his escape from captivity in 1944. It has, however, better claims to fame than this dubious interlude, including a Gothic **cathedral** with a handsome Renaissance doorway and important paintings and sculpture, and the **Palazzo Fantoni**. This is the seat of a learned body whose library, the Biblioteca Ateneo, has several thousand historic volumes, including a number of incunabula (books printed before 1500).

The riviera northward from the town as far as **Gardone★★** is particularly attractive. Just outside the town is the **Vittoriale★** estate, which belonged to the poet Gabriele D'Annunzio (1863-1938). The museum, housed in his neo-Classical villa, La Priora, contains memorabilia relating to his turbulent life.

Limone sul Garda clings to the steep hills adjoining Lake Garda, but most of the citrus groves which gave the village its name have been replaced with buildings.

Limone sul Garda★

Groves of citrus trees on the terraces overlooking the lake make this a pleasantly refreshing spot. It is claimed that the first lemon trees in Europe were grown here. At lake level is an attractive historic quarter.

Riva del Garda★

The second largest town on the lake after Desenzano, Riva shares with its near neighbour, **Torbole**, one of the most dramatic sites – a small area of flat land between towering cliffs, as the lake comes to its narrowest point. It is an elegant and sophisticated place, catering for affluent tourists. For so small a town (the population is a little over 13 000), Riva is exceptionally rich in historical remains. The dominant building is the **Rocca**, a moated castle built in the 12C by the ubiquitous Scaliger of Verona and now a **museum**. Other medieval monuments are the 13C clock tower, the **Torre Apponale** (Apponale Tower), the **Palazzo Pretorio** (Palace of the General) of

The Apponale Tower stands out over the roof tops of the popular resort of Riva del Garda.

1370, and the 15C Palazzo Communale. There is an attractive waterfront, with modern cafés and restaurants.

Torbole

The first town in the Trentino, Torbole is a popular summer resort whose bay is particularly favoured by windsurfers and

A windsurfer's paradise, Torbole beach enjoys a dramatic position, dominated by Monte Baldo.

sailing enthusiasts. It is set at the mouth of the Sarca river, tucked in below the mass of **Dosso Casina** (978m/3 208ft).

Malcesine★

The town presents an attractive mixture of history and tourism. The beach is very popular and behind the town a cable-car ascends **Monte Baldo**, with a magnificent **panorama★★★**. Lower down the mountain are pleasant walks through olive groves. Malcesine was also the seat of the Veronese Captains of the Lake, whose palazzo today serves as the town hall. The Scaliger **castle★** was built in the late 13C and is now a **museum**.

Torri di Benaco

The Romans established a *castrum* on this promontory and the Scaliger followed suit in the late 14C with their **castle**, built on the Roman foundations. The church, built of coloured marble, has 15C frescoes.

Garda★

Tucked away below the prominent **Punta San Vigilio★★** (San Vigilio Point), one of Lake Garda's most beautiful spots, Garda is probably the oldest town on the lake. In the town **museum** are rock engravings and there is a prehistoric necropolis on the outskirts. To the south are the remains of the **Rocca Vecchia** (Old Fortress), a Lombard castle.

Bardolino

Apart from giving its name to a red wine (*see* p.105), Bardolino houses a number of historic remains. Particularly important is the chapel of **San Zeno** (9C), built during the Carolingian empire. **San Severo★** is 12C,

with frescoes of the period. There are also
remains of a Scaliger **castle**. There are plenty
of opportunities to sample the famous wines
and to find out more about them at the
Museo del Vino.

Lazise

This was once an important town,
as attested by the 12C Scaliger
castle and the 14C Venetian
custom-house on the quay. The
Venetians maintained a powerful
naval presence here, and it was an
important trading post. Parts of
the town wall survive.

*The colourful
harbour of Lazise
was once the main
Venetian port on
Lake Garda.*

Peschiera del Garda

Situated where the River Mincio
leaves the lake, the town was of
strategic importance and there is
evidence that it was originally
fortified by the Romans. An interesting view
of the town can be obtained from the
walkway along its encircling walls. These
were begun by the Venetians in the mid 16C.
The town, occupied by the Austrians,
suffered a prolonged siege before falling to
the Italians in 1848.

Sirmione★★

In a region of spectacular sites, this is
outstanding. The long peninsula jutting out
from the southern shoreline is so thin that
the creation of a moat has, in effect, turned
the town at its tip into an island.
Approached by a drawbridge, it is almost
entirely traffic-free, making exploring its
streets on foot a pleasant experience. For
the holidaymaker it combines a wide range
of activities: swimming, windsurfing and

Dante once stayed in the 13C moated Scaligera castle in Sirmione.

tennis, as well as offering the usual architectural interests of an ancient town.

The town, with its spa, was a popular resort with the Romans and the poet Catullus built a villa nearby. The excavation site, **Grotte di Catullo****, enjoys a pleasant, wooded location in which the extensive villa ruins, with its own thermal baths and pool complex, can be explored. Near the Grotte, set high on the peninsula, is the Romanesque church of **San Pietro in Mavino**, founded in the 8C, with frescoes dating from the 13C to 16C.

In addition to its attractions as a spa, Sirmione also had strategic importance and the Scaliger lords of Verona built the massive **Rocca Scaligera*** on Roman foundations in the 13C. There is an excellent **view** of the town and peninsula from the central tower. The battlements protect the 15C church of **Santa Maria Maggiore**, which has interesting 15C and 16C frescoes.

Lago di Ledro (Lake Ledro)

About 6km (3.7 miles) inland from the north-western shore of Lake Garda this small, beautiful lake has a fascinating history. Under certain weather conditions when the water level falls, remains of prehistoric lake dwellings become visible. There is an excellent modern **museum** on the eastern shore, displaying pottery and prehistoric finds from the lake dwellings.

THE SMALLER LAKES

The smaller lakes in Piedmont and Lombardy tend to be overshadowed by the glamorous 'Big Four', but they have a particular charm in that they are relatively unexploited. Even the smallest villages have something worth seeing, and their environs are particularly good for walking and camping.

Lago d'Idro (Lake Idro)
Completely ringed by mountains except at its narrow northern end and less than 2km (1.2 miles) wide, this is the most fjord-like of all the lakes. The River Chiese runs through it from north to south, skirting Lake Garda. Lake Idro is famous for its trout fishing. The nearest town of any size is **Lavenone**, just south of the lake on the bank of the Chiese.

Lago d'Iseo★ (Lake Iseo)
This is smaller only by contrast to the more famous 'Big Four', for it is in fact more than 24km (14.9 miles) long and 5km (3 miles) wide, with the largest island of all the Italian lakes, **Monte Isola★★**. The lake is large enough to boast a steamer service, starting from the town of **Sarnico**. The landscape is Alpine but the climate so mild that olives and vines flourish. **Iseo★**, on the southern shore, is a popular holiday resort on the edge of important wetlands, where remains

of prehistoric lake villages have been found. The medieval origins of **Pisogne★**, at the north of the lake, can be seen in the walls and gates around the old town centre. The 15C **Santa Maria della Neve** has 16C **frescoes★** by Romanino da Brescia.

Lago d'Orta★★ (Lake Orta)

One of the highest lakes in the region, at an altitude of 290m (950ft) and a maximum depth of 143m (470ft), Orta is very much a mountain lake, with Il Mottarone separating it from Lake Maggiore. The island of **San Giulio★★**, in the centre, has an ancient **basilica** with a Romanesque sarcophagus and 15C frescoes. **Orta San Giulio★★**, on a peninsula opposite the island, is a charming lakeside town. The **Sacro Monte★** (Holy Hill) headland behind the town is a famous place of pilgrimage. Twenty chapels, each containing costumed statues depicting events in the life of St Francis of Assisi and

The monastery and basilica occupy most of the island of San Giulio, in Lake Orta.

countless frescoes, are arranged on
the lovely wooded hillside. There
are fine **views★★** from the top across
the lake.

Lago di Varese (Lake Varese)

Set in gently undulating countryside
between the city of Varese and Lago
Maggiore, the lake has been badly
polluted in the past but is in the
process of being cleaned up. On the
prettily wooded **Isolina Virginia**
(Virginia Island) the **Museum of the
Villa Onti** displays prehistoric
remains found nearby. There are two other
small lakes in the vicinity, **Monate**, with
prehistoric remains and **Comabbio**. The
area is on the northernmost tip of the **Parco
Lombardo della Valle del Ticino**.

The city of **Varese** is about 3km (2 miles)
from its lake along a secondary road,
sharing the same pleasant, undulating
countryside. With a population of around
90 000, after Como it is the second largest
city in the region. Its situation has made it
popular with Milan commuters – the
numbers of villas in Varese has given it the
sobriquet 'city of gardens'. The **Palazzo
Estense** of the dukes of Modena (1766-1772)
is now the City Hall, with the once private
gardens open to the public, while the **Villa
Mirabello** houses the **Civic Museum**, with an
important collection of prehistoric finds and
an art gallery. The 16C **Basilica of San
Vittore** has a baptistery dating from the 12C.
A popular local excursion is by bus to the
Parco del Campo dei Fiori★★ and the
mountain village of **Sacro Monte★★**, with its
pilgrimage church and superb **views★★** from
the hilltop (*see above*).

*A Classical archway
spans the path
winding up the tree-
clad hillside of
Sacro Monte,
linking the twenty
devotional chapels.*

The Lakeside Villas

Ever since the Roman poet Catullus (87-54 BC) built his villa at Sirmione, on Lake Garda, those sensitive to the beauty of the lakes, and with the wealth to finance their fancy, have built holiday homes on the shores. The grandest perhaps is the Borromeo Palace on Isola Bella, on Lake Maggiore. In the early 17C, Count Carlo Borromeo transformed a naked rock into a garden by shipping tons of earth from the mainland. A splendid palace was added – so splendid that it was not finished until 1958.

Yet the most characteristic villas are those around Lake Como. There are nine major villas, mostly built between the 16C and 18C, of which the most outstanding is Villa Carlotta (*see* p.69). Today, the Villa d'Este, at Cernobbio, is a luxury hotel. It owes its name to the estranged wife of George IV of England. She stayed there in 1815, claiming to be a descendant of the noble Este family of Ferrara. The neo-Classical Villa dell'Olmo, in Como itself, was built in 1782 and has a classic Italian garden from which there are lovely views over Como. Villa Monastero, at Varenna, began life as a Cistercian monastery in 1208 and was turned into a villa in 1569. It has a superb lakeside loggia. Most of the villas are open to the public.

Gardens at Villa Taranto, Pallanza.

Above: Villa Ciani, on Lake Lugano.

THE TRENTINO

A beautiful landscape of lakes, valleys, rivers, woods and small towns, since 1947 its official title and status has been that of the Autonomous Region of Trentino-Alto Adige. Alto Adige (higher Adige) refers to the great river that has created a natural highway through the region. In the north is the Brenner Pass, leading into the heart of Europe: in the south is Lake Garda and the entrance to the Plain of Lombardy. Armies have marched to and fro, from the time of Attila the Hun to Napoleon and Adolf Hitler. The mountainous nature of the landscape has meant that from time to time the fiercely independent natives have been able to wrest a modicum of independence from the current overlord. Today, for instance, although within a unified Italy, the region has been able to claim semi-autonomy, creating its own laws for certain internal matters.

TRENTO★

The story of Trento is bound up with the development of one of the most extraordinary figures from the Middle Ages – the militant Prince-Bishop who, with a crucifix in one hand and a sword in the other, ruled like a despot.

The city, lying in a cat's-cradle of valleys where the roads from Garda, Verona and Venice cross those to the Dolomites and the Brenner, has been of vital strategic importance throughout its history. The Romans naturally placed their hand upon it, guarding as it did the great Roman military road, the Claudia Augusts Padana, and turned it into a *Municipium*. As early as the second half of the 5C it was the capital of a diocese, the Christian organisation based on a Roman division, with the bishop as effective ruler. The Holy Roman Emperors, invariably German despite their title, realised the importance of keeping open this vital route south to their titular empire. In 1027, the Emperor Conrad II conferred the title of prince upon the bishop and his successors ruled as Prince-Bishops for about 800 years, until the coming of Napoleon in 1801. The city was the seat of the long-running **Council of Trent** (1545-1563) which sought to reform the Church after the Protestant reaction created by Martin Luther. Many of the splendid public buildings were designed to impress the important visitors attending the Council. Trento was ceded by Austria to Italy in 1918.

Detail of a ceiling fresco in the Castle of Good Council, Trento, once the home of the Prince-Bishops.

Although Trento is a large commercial city of over 100 000 people, its position with a river at its feet and mountains at its back makes it attractively compact and with the freshness of a country town. Look out for the frescoes, both inside and outside buildings, which are a characteristic of the city. There are some interesting murals on the 15C **Casa Bazzani**, close to the cross-roads known as the **Canton**.

Castello del Buon Consiglio★
(Castle of Good Council)
The seat of the Prince-Bishops, with building going on continuously for over 400 years from the 13C to the 17C, this is undoubtedly the showpiece of Trento and is today an

important museum. There is a clear-cut
distinction between the medieval northern
section and the Renaissance southern. The
frescoes are outstanding. In the courtyard is
an immense mural of the Emperor
Charlemagne and the Prince-Bishops of
Trento, painted in 1535 to emphasise the
legitimacy and power of the bishops. In the
Torre dell'Aquila (Eagle Tower) is the
wonderful *Cycle of the Months*, looking as fresh
as when they were painted around 1400, and
showing a fascinating array of local scenes.

Duomo★ (Cathedral)
Built almost entirely of marble, the
construction of the cathedral extended over
three centuries, from early 13C to early 16C,
and incorporates Romanesque and
Renaissance features. The decrees of the
Council of Trent were promulgated in the
cathedral. In the cobbled **Piazza del Duomo★**
outside is the 18C **Neptune Fountain**.

Palazzo Pretorio (Palace of the General)
Situated on the Piazza del Duomo, this was
originally the palace of the bishops in their
role of princes. It is today the **Museo
Diocesano★** (Diocesan Museum), exhibiting
art treasures from local churches.

Santa Maria Maggiore
The church was built in a pure Renaissance
style at a very early date, 1520, considering
how far north it is from the origins of the
Renaissance in Tuscany. Many of the sessions
of the Council of Trent were held here.

Torre Civica (Civic Tower)
This late medieval tower was built over a
Roman town gate, Porta Veronensis.

THE LAKES OF TRENTINO

There are an incredible 297 lakes in the Trentino region. They range from majestic Lake Garda (*see* p.72), largest of all Italian lakes, to beautiful little **Lago di Cei**, covered with the water-lilies from which it gets its dialect name. As you travel north, so the mountains crowd round, frequently mirrored in the clear water. The five briefly described below are within easy reach of Trento.

Lago di Caldonazzo and Lago di Levico

Both lakes are about 13km/8 miles south-east of Trento on the S 47.

Situated on the natural highway of the Valsugana, the lakes have been colonised since the time of the Romans and there are many historical remains. Caldonazzo is the largest lake entirely in the Trentino and is separated from Levico by a ridge. The two together form a popular holiday resort, much favoured by the people of Trento. Caldonazzo has good beaches and bathing facilities, together with sailing and fishing. Levico has an internationally famous spa.

Lago di Molveno★★

40km/25 miles north-west of Trento. Leave Trento on the S 45b, and turn left at Sarche along the S 237, branching right along the S 421 to the lake.

One of the most dramatic of sites, backed up as it is by

The mighty Dolomites dwarf the settlement of Molveno, which nestles at the mouth of the mountain pass.

the rugged mass of the **Brenta Dolomites**★★★, which resembles the pinnacles and towers of a Gothic cathedral. The village of **Molveno**★, with the church of **San Vigilio** (14C), nestles in the mouth of the pass leading up into the mountains. The lake's magic has survived even the building of a dam for hydro-electric purposes. Dotted around are the forts built by the Austrians against the Napoleonic invasions.

Lago di Toblino★

11km/7 miles west of Trento along the S 45b.
The lake is in the middle of a valley, carved out by glacial action, and surrounded by woods and vineyards. Jutting out is a small peninsula on which is a **castle**, once the summer palace of the Prince-Bishops of Trento, surrounded by gardens. Part of the castle is now a restaurant.

The Trentino has many little-known treasures, hidden from the usual tourist trail. This gem, with its remarkable emerald green waters, is Lake Tovel.

Lago di Tovel★★★

About 50km/30 miles north of Trento. Leave the city going north on either the A 22 or S 12, turning west onto the S 43 at San Michele all'Adige. Bear left onto the pretty minor road to the lake, via Sporminore, Denno, Flavon or Tuenno.

Set at an altitude of 1 178m (3 865ft) in an amphitheatre of towering white cliffs, the waters of this small, triangular lake are an astonishing emerald green. Fir trees crowd down to the shoreline, which is dotted with little gravel beaches.

THE CASTLES OF TRENTINO

The unsettled history of this border region is characterised by a remarkable number of rural castles, mostly defending the passes and backed up by small towns.

(Those listed here allow public access without formality and are either on, or easily accessible from, the main A 22 Verona-Trento road, running north through the Valle d'Adige parallel to Lake Garda. Other castles require booking in advance by groups.)

Pergine

10km/6 miles east of Trento, via the S 47.
Unlike most Trentino castles, which have been altered again and again over the centuries, Pergine maintains its appearance of a medieval fortified Alpine manor. Its origins are unknown, but probably date back to the Lombard period.

Although the castle is private property there is a public restaurant established in the Great Hall, providing visitors with the most unusual experience of dining where the lord of the manor once dined with his people.

The castle of Sabbionara d'Avio must have presented a formidable and daunting prospect for medieval attackers.

Sabbionara d'Avio

28km/17 miles north of Verona, just off the main road.

This is the first castle encountered travelling up the Valle d'Adige from Verona. Originally built by the Castelbarco family in the 12C, it was extended in the 14C in the style made fashionable by the Scaliger of Verona. It passed through various hands, including those of the Venetians and the Prince-Bishops, and since 1977 has been the property of a Trust, the Fund for the Italian Environment, which has carried out excellent restoration. Particularly important are the 14C Veronese Gothic frescoes.

Rovereto

21km/13 miles south of Trento.

The castle is built on the site of a prehistoric hill-fort, which in turn was developed by the Romans. The present castle was built by the Venetians between the 15C and 16C to hold out against the new weapon of artillery. It was successively occupied by Napoleonic and Austrian troops. The castle is the seat of the **Italian Historical War Museum**, dedicated to the events of the First World War.

Stenico

15km/9 miles west of Trento.

The frescoes of the Torre dell'Aquila in the Castello del Buon Consiglio, in Trento (*see* p.87), provide an excellent picture of this castle. Perched on the side of a heavily wooded ravine a few minutes' walk from the little town, Stenico shows a remarkable range of architectural styles from Romanesque to Renaissance, the latter characterised by a beautiful loggia. The 13C chapel of San Martino contains a cycle of Romanesque frescoes. Recently restored, the rooms have been furnished from the Provincial Art Museum Collection.

Thun

5km/3 miles north of Mezzo-Corona, off the main road.

Castel Thun is the physical expression of the power of a single family. For nearly 500 years, the Thuns ruled supreme over the Valle di Non and Valle di Sole, first with the title of Baron, then as Counts of the Empire. In the early 13C, they acquired the primitive **Castello di Belvesino** and over the years turned it into a sumptuous residence. The approach is through a formal garden, then over a drawbridge protected by five towers to the main body of the castle, a square five-storeyed block arranged around a courtyard. The furnishing of the rooms are historical, including a library of some 10 000 volumes. On the second floor is the Bishop's Room, in which the last Prince-Bishop of Trento died.

GETTING ABOUT ON THE LAKES

The easiest and certainly the most attractive way of getting around the lakes themselves is by water. Como, Maggiore, Lugano and Iseo have the state-operated Lake Navigation Company, whose craft function as both ferries and pleasure boats. In addition, there are numerous independent companies operating on most of the lakes. Some operators still use the old-fashioned paddle steamers. Journeys can be surprisingly long, so be sure to allocate plenty of time. A round trip on Como, for example, will take about six hours by ordinary steamer, while on Maggiore even the fast-moving hydrofoil takes two hours to travel the length from Arona to Locarno. Nevertheless, boat tours provide a relaxed and scenic means of sightseeing.

The hydrofoil saves time but is more expensive and a less attractive means of travel, as one is enclosed and confined to a seat. The larger craft have bars and restaurants and there are also evening

A relaxed and enjoyable way of exploring the lakes is aboard one of the many tour boats.

cruises, combined with dinner. When travelling on Lake Lugano it is advisable to have a passport with you, particularly if you intend to land on the Swiss side. This also applies if you plan to visit Locarno, on Lake Maggiore.

The tourist offices (APT) in the major lake cities will provide timetables, itineraries and tariffs. It is possible to obtain all-day tickets, which will allow you to hop from boat to boat, and to stop off and explore the towns and villages around the lake. Motorboats can be hired on Lake Garda for those who wish to explore the lake independently.

WEATHER

On the Po Plain itself the climate can be extreme – cold in winter and in summer often shrouded in a thick, greyish fog caused by the high humidity. In the cities the dog days are in August, when everyone who can do so gets out into the countryside. The Lakes themselves tend to be more temperate, the large sheets of water – although frequently shrouded in mists – act as storage radiators in winter and raise temperatures, and the mountains shield them from more extreme weather. In summer, the Lakes reduce the temperature by a few degrees, and there are refreshing breezes which blow predictably down the valleys – a bonus for windsurfers and sailors. The temperature range is around 5°C (40°F) in January, rising to the mid 20°sC (70°sF) in July, with the more western lakes tending to be cooler. Sudden thunderstorms are common in summer.

What makes the region particularly

interesting is that an Alpine climate meets a Mediterranean one here, creating some of the most beautiful gardens in Italy, together with a wide range of fruit and vegetables. Undoubtedly, the best times of the year for a visit are in spring, before the crowds arrive and with the first wonderful blooming of flowers, and in autumn, just before the *vendémmia* (grape harvest) in late September. The superb colours of the autumnal countryside are well worth the risk of rainfall in October.

CALENDAR OF EVENTS

Italy has no fewer than nine national holidays or festivals (*see* p.122). In addition, every city and most towns and villages will have their own local festivals, of which lists can be obtained from the tourist office (APT). The following is a selection of events occurring in Lombardy. Dates can vary within a week or so.

January: (6) Three Kings Procession, Milan; (31) Boat Festival, San Giulio, Lake Orta

February: Carnivals at Arcoz, Bagolino (Brescia), Bormio, Milan, Schignano (Como), Verona (Bacchanalian Carnival of the Gnocco)

March: Sant'Ambrogio Carnival, Milan; autumn fashion collections, Milan

April: (9-10) Pageantry to commemorate the Oath of the Lombard League, Bergamo

End April/1st week May: Flower Festival, Orta San Giulio

May: Palio del Carroccio, Legnano, Milan

June: (4) Navigli Festival, Milan; (6) Festival of San Gerardo, Monza; (23) Festival Comacina; (last Sunday) Festival Popolare del Lago di Garda, Limone sul Garda;

Festival Cusiano di Musica Antica, Orta San Giulio

July-August: Opera season in the Arena and theatre (Shakespeare Festival) in the Teatro Romano, Verona; open-air theatre in the Vittoriale, in Gardone

July: Estival Jazz and music festivals, Lugano

August: Firework Festival, Omegna, Lake Orta; Navigli Festival, Milan; International Film Festival, Locarno

End August-September: Settimane Musicali, Stresa

September: (2) Horse palio, Isola Dovarese, Cremona; Italian Grand Prix, Monza; Il Grappolo d'Oro (grape harvest festival), Ghiuro, Sondrio; Festa dell'Uva, wine festivals held on last weekend of the month throughout the wine region, such as Bardolino

Boats come in all shapes and sizes.

October: (1st Sunday) Festa della Madonna del Rosario, Montodine, Cremona; spring fashion collections, Milan

December-April: Stagione di Prosa (theatrical performances), Brescia

December-July: La Scala opera season (opens 7 December), Milan

All Year: Opera in Donizetti Theatre, Bergamo

ACCOMMODATION

For information before you go on all aspects of staying in the region, refer to the *Michelin Red Guide Italia*. This guide, which is updated every year, offers a selection of hotels, from the simplest to the most luxurious, classified by district and according to comfort.

The Italian government classifies hotels from one to five stars, and most towns and resorts in the Italian Lakes region are well supplied with accommodation in all classes.

Prices vary between lakes and resorts, but as a guide you can expect to pay (per double room, with bath):

5 star: over L500 000
4 star: L300-500 000
3 star: L200-300 000
2 star: L100-200 000
1 star: under L100 000

Hotels located on the lakes' shores are very much in demand, and it is advisable to reserve accommodation well in advance of your visit; this also applies to Milan. Away from the lakes, simpler, cheaper hotels can be found. Lake Como probably boasts the most luxurious hotels of all.

A popular alternative to hotels in the Lakes region is *Agriturismo*, self-catering (usually) accommodation on a working farm. Home-grown produce is often available and prices are reasonable. For further information contact the head office at Corso V Emanuele, 101, 00186 Roma, ☎ **(06) 6512 342**, or the Regional Office for the area you want to visit (*see* **Tourist Information Offices**).

A scattering of youth hostels, known in Italy as *ostelli della gioventù*, can be found in the region, including Milan, Bergamo and Como. For details of hostels and how to book, apply to the Italian Youth Hostel Association (AIG) at Via Cavour 44, 00184 Rome ☎ **(06) 4871 152**. An international membership card is required, which can sometimes be purchased on the spot.

Recommendations

Milan
Over L800 000
Four Seasons (Via Gesù 8, 20121 Milano
☎ (02) 770 88 Fax 7708 50 00) One of
Milan's most luxurious hotels, centrally
located in the heart of the city's most
fashionable district, near Montenapoleone.
L260 000-340 000
Hotel Regina (Via Cesare Correnti 13, 20123
Milano ☎ (02) 5810 69 13 Fax 5810 70 33)
Comfortable hotel installed in an 18C
building situated in the historic centre, near
the Basilica of San Lorenzo Maggiore.
Hotel Regency (Via Arimondi 12, 20155
Milano ☎ (02) 3921 60 21 Fax 3921 77 34)
Early-20C town house in the Sempione
quarter, north-west of the historic centre.
L120 000-150 000
Antica Locanda Solferino (Via Castelfidardo 2
☎ (02) 657 01 29 Fax 657 13 61) This small
hotel, offering simple accommodation, is
located just north of the Brera district,
renowned for its restaurants and cafés.

On Lake Maggiore
Colmegna
(2.5km/1.5 miles north of Luino)
L140 000-190 000
Camin Hotel Colmegna (Via Palazzi 1,
Colmegna, 21016 Luino ☎ (0332) 51 08 55
Fax 53 7226) This 21-room hotel is set within
a park on the shores of Lake Maggiore.
Isola dei Pescatori (Isole Borromee)
L160 000-230 000
Verbano (Via Ugo Ara 12, 28049 Stresa
☎ (0323) 304 08 Fax 331 29) This tranquil
small hotel (12 rooms), located on the
southern tip of Isola dei Pescatori, has lovely

views of nearby Isola Bella.

Cannobio
L120 000-180 000

Pironi (Via Marconi 35 – in the historic centre – ☎ (0323) 706 24 Fax 721 84) This small inn (12 rooms), installed in a Renaissance monastery in Connobio's historic centre, exudes a unique charm and intimacy.

Ghiffa
L115 000-160 000

Park Hotel Paradiso (Via Guglielmo Marconi 20 ☎ (0323) 595 48) Guests at this small hotel (15 rooms) will be charmed by this lovely art nouveau villa, set in a small garden (heated pool) offering lovely views of the lake and the surrounding mountains.

Lake trout is understandably a speciality of the region.

On Lake Garda
Gardone Riviera
L300 000-540 000

Villa Fiordaliso (Corso Zanardelli 150 ☎ (0365) 201 58 Fax 29 00 11) This renowned gourmet restaurant, set in a lovely villa on the banks of Lake Garda, offers six rooms, one of which was reputedly favoured by Mussolini for trysts with Claretta Petacci.

Garda

Locanda San Vigilio (San Vigilio ☎ (045) 725 66 88) This charming villa is located in San Vigilio on the east shore of Lake Garda.

On Lake Como
Lenno
L130 000-170 000

Hotel San Giorgio (☎ (0344) 404 15 Fax 415 91) Hotel (26 rooms) with terraced gardens extending to the shores of Lake Como.

On Lake Orta
Orta San Giulio
L230 000-480 000
Villa Crespi (Via Fava 18, 28016 Novara ☎ (0322) 91 19 02 Fax 91 19 19) Known primarily as a gourmet restaurant, this 19C residence with exotic touches also offers six rooms and eight suites.

Verona
L170 000-230 000
Hotel Bologna (Via Alberto Mario 18, 37121 Verona ☎ (045) 800 68 30 Fax 801 06 02) Pleasant hotel with 31 rooms; restaurant *Rubiani* on the Piazzetta Scalette Rubiani, nearby.
De' Capuleti (Via del Pontiere 26, 37122 Verona ☎ (045) 800 01 54 Fax 803 29 70) Hotel (without restaurant); 42 rooms.

Trento
L120 000-170 000
Villa Madruzzo (at Cognola, 3km from Trento; Via Ponte Alto 26 ☎ (0461) 98 62 20 Fax 98 63 61) Pleasant hotel installed in a 19C villa (51 rooms) with a shaded garden.

Bergamo
L100 000-140 000
Il Gourmet (Via San Vigilio 1, 24129 Bergamo ☎ (035) 437 30 04 Fax 437 30 04) Located in Bergamo's spectacular Upper Town, this restaurant, appreciated for its panoramic terrace, offers 10 moderately-priced rooms.

FOOD AND DRINK

The regionalism which causes so many political headaches to Italy is a delight for the visitor. Every major city, and almost every village or small town, will have some speciality which is difficult or impossible to get anywhere else. If you order ordinary wine (*vino da tavola*) in a restaurant, and the locality produces only white wine, then you will get white wine unless you order a more expensive branded bottled wine.

Specialities in Lombardy reflect the wide range of its topography. Trentino offers snails. Around the lakes fish is widely served, mostly trout or perch. Especially highly regarded is the carp from Lake Garda, known as *carpione*, although this can also refer to the way the fish is prepared (fish stew). *Risotto con pesce persico* (a rice dish with perch) has been served around Como since the days of the Romans. Higher up in the mountains, preserved meats and sausages made with boar meat (*cinghiale*) are popular. Apart from the ubiquitous pasta, a staple throughout Lombardy is *polenta*, made from maize flour and eaten with a variety of dishes.

The fast-food culture has been largely kept at bay. The nearest thing to it which Italians will recognise is the *tavola calda* (literally 'hot table'). This serves traditional food but more quickly as it is prepared in advance, without the trappings of a restaurant. The cover charge (*coperto*) covers unlimited amount of bread and often *grissini* (bread sticks), condiments and a clean tablecloth, even if only made of paper. Responding to tourist needs, most restaurants offer fixed-price meals (*menu turistico*) usually consisting of two courses with wine.

Recommendations

Italian restaurants tend to be grouped together, and one of the great pleasures of eating out is to stroll along a street where they have accumulated and pick one out. Those listed below are suggestions, arranged by locality.

Arona

Taverna del Pittore (Piazza del Popolo 39 ☎ (0322) 243366) A very good restaurant, though quite expensive. Has a veranda offering a nice view of the Rocca di Angera. Among their specialities try the Fegato grasso d'oca (fois gras) or one of the fish dishes.
Del Barcaiolo (Piazza del Popolo 20/23 ☎ (0322) 243388) A typical 'taverna'.

Bellagio

Ristorante Bilacus (Via Serbelloni 32 ☎ (031) 950480) Moderately priced meals in a charming garden.

Bergamo

Taverna Colleoni dell'Angelo (Piazza Vecchia 7 ☎ (035) 232596) Atmospheric and friendly, in the Upper Town; expensive.

Relaxing after a day's sightseeing at a pavement café in Stresa, Lake Maggiore.

Brescia
La Sosta (Via S. Martino della Battaglia 20 ☎ (030) 295603) Set in a converted 17C building, with extensive menu.

Cernobbio
Ristorante Cenobio (Via Regina 18 ☎ (031) 512710) Good menu; restaurant with open veranda.

Como
Ristorante Imbarcadero (Piazza Cavour 20 ☎ (031) 270166) Elegant, up-market dining on the lakeside piazza.

Comacina
La locanda dell Isola (☎ (0344) 56755) A delightful island setting, with set price meals (limited menu).

Erba (on the Como-Lecco road)
Castello di Casiglio (Via Cantu, 19 ☎ (031) 627288) A medieval castle in a garden. Not cheap, but offering international as well as regional cuisine.

Milan
Probably the most expensive city for eating out in all Italy.
Savini (Galleria Vittorio Emanuele II ☎ (02) 7200 3433) At the top end of the market. For more modest pockets, try:
Trattoria all'antica (Via Montevideo 4 ☎ (02) 5810 4860) Offers regional cuisine at moderate prices.

Sarnico
Al Desco (Piazza XX Settembre 19 ☎ (035) 910740) Good fish restaurant.

Sirmione
The Signori (Via Romagnoli 23 ☎ (030) 916017) With a pleasant ambiance.

Verona
Bottega del Vino (Via Scudo di Francia 3 ☎ (045) 8004535) As its name indicates, this specialises in wine, with hundreds of types.

Wines

Italy has an astonishing variety of wines, with each village – indeed, each farmhouse – producing something slightly different from all the rest. The wine served in a city restaurant has very likely been produced in the proprietor's own vineyard and will not have a label. Recently the Italian government introduced the DOCG system (*Denominazione di Origine Controllata e Garantita*), which indicates wine of a guaranteed vintage. It is a useful but not exclusive system, with many excellent wines being produced without a DOCG label. A fascinating, relatively recent development has been the *enoteca*, a kind of showcase for wine where you can taste and buy a glass, a bottle or even a case.

Most wines are still produced by relatively small vineyards who welcome visitors to wine-tasting in the season. Country roads will sprout handwritten signs indicating a *fattoria* nearby. Although there is no obligation to buy, it is a matter of courtesy to do so. Apart from the opportunity to taste wine, many of the farmhouses are of considerable antiquity and of great interest.

The light wines of the **Veneto**, particularly those around Lake Garda and near Verona, have become popular abroad so are instantly recognisable. All are meant to be drunk 'young', that is, within a year or so of their production. **Bardolino**, on the south-eastern shore of Lake Garda, a charming little town in its own right with an ancient Scaliger castle, has given its name to a red wine. The **Valpolicella** district on the hills inland from the lake produces not only another red wine but also the beautiful pink marble, known as *rosso di Verona* because it was much used for

Verona's monuments. **Soave**, a popular white wine, has been named after a small fortified town just off the road from Verona to Venice. **Bassano del Grappa**, on the road from Venice to Trento, is famous for *grappa*, the fiery Italian liqueur, but it is now widely produced throughout the country.

The *vendémmia*, or grape harvest, which takes place in late September or early October, is a remarkable experience. The grapes may be transported now by trucks rather than ox cart, but the busy activity and the sense of abundance could belong to a medieval painting.

SHOPPING

The strong spirit of locality that underlies everything in Italy, from politics to food, also influences what you can buy and where. Italy is still very much the land of the individual

Milan is one of Europe's leading fashion centres.

craftsman, working alone or with his family, frequently selling his wares himself. Many localities will have some speciality, either in marketing or in manufacture.

For **fashion**, what better place to look than Milan, where houses like Armani, Gucci and Versace were founded. Head for Via Montenapoleone and its neighbouring shopping streets and you will find world famous boutiques side by side. For **silk** go to Como, where they have been making it for the past 500 years.

Antiques feature in virtually every city – but don't forget that this is a nation of supreme artists who can turn out Michelangelos that could fool Michelangelo! Remember, too, that genuine works of art need an export licence. Visitors looking for something a little different to take home should browse in the local antique markets.

Handicrafts are widespread and varied. The Trentino specialises in metalwork and, under the Germanic influence, exquisitely carved woodwork. Ceramics and leather-work are genuinely local artworks. The shores of Lake Maggiore are rich in craft shops. At Pallanza you can buy violins and lutes made by local craftsmen. The villages along Lake Iseo produce woodwork of high quality, as well as wickerwork baskets, copper and wrought-iron work. Markets everywhere are living institutions. Most will have their wares priced – Italians are not really into haggling – but where they are not priced it is up to you to decide what you really want to spend.

Where Italy generally does excel is in its **olive oils**, and there are shops dedicated solely to their sale. The olive oil from Lake Garda is highly esteemed; for the best, look for '*extra virgine*' olive oil.

ENTERTAINMENT AND NIGHTLIFE

There is such a lot of action that it is best to visit the local tourist office (APT) to see what is available. In addition, the local newspapers of the four great cities covered in this book provide detailed listings.

The two great showpieces in the area are, of course, the **music festivals** in La Scala, in Milan, and the **opera** spectaculars in the Arena, in Verona. La Scala runs a virtually continual programme, with opera from December to July and symphony concerts from September to November. In Verona, the Arena opera season runs through July and August, with *Aida* almost invariably top of the bill. Rock concerts are also staged in the Arena. For both La Scala and the Arena it is best to book well beforehand – before arriving in Italy if possible.

This modern-day audience, enjoying the opera in Verona's Arena, is witnessing a less bloody spectacle than their Roman forbears.

But these two are only the icing on the cake. In Verona there are also the **ballets** and **drama** staged in the Roman theatre across the river. Milan has a number of venues, including churches, where concerts are given. There is also the delightful **Teatro delle Marionette** (Puppet Theatre) where, if you are lucky, you may see one of the traditional Sicilian puppet plays.

The larger towns and cities are abuzz with **bars** – the 'piano bar' with its gently tinkling piano is enjoying great popularity, a civilised compromise between the raucous **disco** (of which there are any number) and the solitary corner café.

Don't forget the **festivals** (*see* p.96). Virtually every village will have its patron saint who is honoured with lights and bands and processions once a year. In Milan, Sant'Ambrogio is celebrated with a tremendous carnival in March. If there is no saint to be honoured, then a local custom will do, such as the Flower Festival at Orto San Giulio or the commemoration of the 12C Lombard League at Bergamo.

Finally, there is the *passegiata* – everywhere, from the largest city to the smallest hamlet. It is the time of the day, usually around 6pm, when all the inhabitants of a small town, or a quarter as in Milan or Brescia, dress up and stroll along a recognised route.

SPORTS

This is the playground of Italy – indeed of Europe – and there is everything here from rigorous self-testing mountaineering to lazing beside swimming pools with long cool drinks. You can play golf, go horse-riding or, if your nerves are strong enough, try hanggliding. In winter there is skiing, in summer snorkelling. A rapidly growing industry is *agriturismo*. At its simplest, this is a room in a farmhouse, but more and more farms will provide rural sports such as riding and fishing in addition to accommodation and food.

It is well worth visiting the local state tourist office (APT) to find out what is on offer. In general, Lake Garda is the more heavily developed area – some 15 million people, mostly from abroad, visit it annually – with emphasis on commercial organisations. The National Reserves, like Monte Bondone just 12km (7.5 miles) from Trento, offer tranquillity with amenities within easy reach.

Mountain sports Mountain bikes have become immensely popular. Bikes can be hired at local sporting shops together with planned itineraries, some of which include a cable-car service like the one from Malcesine on Lake Garda to the peak of Monte Baldo. For walkers, the main lake venues have waymarked paths up into the hills. Serious walkers can plan week-long trips through the national parks, staying at refuges overnight.

Water sports Since 1984 rigorous regulations covering safety, ecological protection and tourism have come into force on the lakes, with substantial fines for offences. If you are hiring a motor boat make sure you are aware of regulations concerning speed, forbidden areas and waste disposal – it is even necessary to wash a boat's keel before putting it in the water. Divers must have a buoy indicating their position. Fishing needs an annual licence. But the regulations are designed to enhance the amenities for all. Swimming is possible from most of the lakeside beaches. Pianello del Lario, on the west shore of Lake Como, is the home of the Como Sailing Club. The predictability of the winds on Como make it particularly suitable for learners and the Club runs courses. The triangular area between Riva, Malcesine and Limone on Lake Garda is a windsurfers' paradise. Motorboats, apart from the public services, are forbidden in the area. You can hire

Hiking in the Italian Lakes is a pure delight, whether on a waymarked walk or a full-scale serious hike – the views are guaranteed.

equipment, including the compulsory lifejackets, locally.

Theme parks Italians are particularly good at gilding the lily. In case the superb scenery, the wonderful food and the rich history are not sufficient, a number of additional attractions have been created. Most varied is the amusement park **Gardaland**, at Castelnuovo del Garda (Peschiera exit on the motorway), which has everything from a Wild West Village, complete with cowpokes, to laser shows at night. An entirely different theme is the **Parco Giardino Sigurtà** (Sigurtà Garden Park). Forty years ago Count Doctor Carlo Sigurta, using his rights to draw water from the River Mincio, began to create this garden on a barren hillside, 8km (5 miles) from Peschiera. Today, it covers 125 acres. **Il Mondi di Caneva**, at Lazise, offers a variety of water sports for everyone from small children to adults. It has proved so popular that another has opened in Inzago, between Bergamo and Milan.

THE BASICS

Before You Go

Visitors entering Italy should have a full passport valid to cover the period in which they will be travelling. No visa is required for members of EU countries. Citizens of the Republic of Ireland, the United States, Canada, Australia and New Zealand can stay in Italy for up to three months without a visa. No vaccinations are necessary.

Getting There

By Air: The most convenient airport for visitors to the Lake Como and Lake Maggiore region is Milan. Malpensa Airport (50km/31 miles north-west of Milan) handles international flights, while Linate Airport (7km/4.5 miles east of Milan) handles domestic and European flights. Direct scheduled flights from the UK are operated by Alitalia, ☎ **(0171) 602 711** and British Airways, ☎ **0345 222111**. There are direct flights from the US to Milan and Rome.

Visitors to the Lake Garda region can fly to Verona from the UK with British Airways.

By Car: To take a car into Italy, a vehicle registration document, a full driving licence and insurance papers are required. The European motorway network makes Northern Italy easy to get to, although tolls in Switzerland are expensive. Piedmont is crossed by the A 21 and the A 26 and the region of the Lombard lakes is well connected by the A 8, A 9 and A 4 motorways. Veneto is easily accessible via the A 22 and the A 4 and Trentino is bisected by the A 22.

See also **Driving** and **Car Hire**

By Coach: Eurolines runs regular bus services to Milan, Bergamo and Verona from the UK and other European countries. Information and bookings in the UK can be made from 52 Grosvenor Gardens, London SW1W OAU ☎ **(0171) 730 8235**.

By Train: Milan is easily reached by rail from the UK, travelling via Eurostar to Paris then taking an overnight train (about 10 hours). Milan is connected by rail to a number of the lakes and towns in the region, including Lake Maggiore, Lake Como, Bergamo, Brescia, Lake Garda and Verona. *See also* **Transport** CIT offices act as agents for Italian State Railways and can be contacted at:

UK Marco Polo House, 3-5 Lansdowne Road, Croydon,

Surrey ☎ (0181) 686 0677
USA 342 Madison Avenue,
Suite 207, New York, NY 10173
☎ (212) 697 2497

Arriving

Within three days of arriving in
Italy, all foreign nationals must
register with the police. If you
are staying in a hotel, the man-
agement will normally attend
to this formality, but strictly
speaking the visitor is responsi-
ble for checking that it has
been carried out.

*A charming typical cobbled street
in Salita Serbelloni, Lake Como.*

A-Z

Accidents and Breakdowns

In the case of a breakdown, dial ☎ 116 from the nearest phone box and the operator will send an ACI (Italian Automobile Club) service vehicle. A red warning triangle should be placed 50m behind the vehicle, and the hazard warning lights switched on. In the event of an accident, exchange names, addresses and insurance details. To contact the police or ambulance, dial ☎ 113. There are emergency telephones at 1km intervals along the motorway (autostrade).

When travelling in a hire car, contact the rental firm in the event of an accident or breakdown. Spare parts and service facilities for Italian makes of cars are simple to find, but all major towns have agencies for most other makes. *See also* **Driving**

Accommodation see p.97

Airports see Getting There p.112

Banks

Banks are open from 8.30am-1.30pm, Monday to Friday, and sometimes for one hour in the afternoon, usually 3-4pm. They are closed at weekends and on national holidays.

Tourists can change money at main railway stations and airports, and travellers' cheques and cheques can be changed at most hotels, although the exchange rate may not be very favourable.

Bicycles

Bicycles can be hired in most Italian towns and resorts and are a very pleasant way of getting around; bear in mind the heat of summer, however, and the topography of the area you wish to explore.

Breakdowns see Accidents

Camping

This is one of the most attractive areas for enjoying the outdoor life, with many sites located very near the lakes;

those away from them are quieter and cheaper. The sites range from the simple to the very sophisticated, and prices vary accordingly. For full details of all the sites in this region, and booking forms, apply to the Italian Camping Federation (Federcampeggio), Castella Postale 23, 50041 Calenzano, Firenze ☎ **(055) 88 2391**. Otherwise ask for information from the Italian Tourist Office in your own country (*see* **Tourist Information Offices**).

Car Hire

Milan and the region's main towns and resorts are well served by both international and local car-hire agencies, and airlines and tour operators offer fly-drive arrangements. Car hire in conjunction with train travel is also available through some of the major car hire companies.

Weekly rates with unlimited mileage offer the best deal; these include breakdown service and basic insurance, but you are advised to take out a collision damage waiver and personal accident insurance in addition. The small local firms generally offer the cheapest rates, but they can only be booked locally.

Most hire companies restrict hire of cars to drivers over 21 (some stipulate a minimum age of 23). Drivers must have held their full licence for at least a year. With the exception of Avis, there is an upper age limit of 60-65. Unless paying by credit card, a substantial cash deposit is required. Full details of the different hire schemes can be obtained from tourist offices. *See also* **Driving, Accidents and Breakdowns** and **Tourist Information Offices**

Children

Apart from the permanent funfairs found in many of the larger towns, children's attractions as such tend to be concentrated around Lake Garda. The many boat trips available on the lakes are always a popular option. Look out too for travelling circuses. The following attractions should appeal to children:
Gardaland, Peschiera. A huge theme park reminiscent of Disneyland.
Parco Minitalia, Capriate San Gervasio. Scaled-down version of Italy, with miniature train.
Parco della Preistoria, Rivolta d'Adda. Train ride through wooded valley populated by model dinosaurs.
Parco Natura Viva, near Lazise. Leisure park with concrete dinosaurs.

Villa Pallavicino, Stresa, Lake Maggiore. Park and children's zoo.

Churches *see* **Religion**

Climate *see* **p.95**

Clothing

Spring and autumn are warm and pleasant times of the year to visit the Italian Lakes, and during those months light clothes can be worn in the day, with an extra sweater or jacket for the evenings and cooler days. Around the large lakes, sudden cloudbursts are not unusual, so be prepared. Summers are slightly cooler than in most Mediterranean areas, and winters somewhat warmer.

Most Italian clothing measurements are standard throughout Europe but different from those in the UK and the US. The following are examples:

Women's sizes

UK	8	10	12	14	16	18
Italy	38	40	42	44	46	48
US	6	8	10	12	14	16

Men's suits

UK/US	36	38	40	42	44	46
Italy	46	48	50	52	54	56

Men's shirts

UK/US	14	14.5	15	15.5	16	16.5	17
Italy	36	37	38	39/40	41	42	43

Men's shoes

UK	7	7.5	8.5	9.5	10.5	11
Italy	41	42	43	44	45	46
US	8	8.5	9.5	10.5	11.5	12

Women's shoes

UK	4.5	5	5.5	6	6.5	7
Italy	38	38	39	39	40	41
US	6	6.5	7	7.5	8	8.5

The spacious Piazza Bra viewed from the Arena, Verona.

Consulates

Australia
Via Borgogna 2, 20122 Milan
☎ (02) 777 041

Canada
Via Vittorio Pisani 19, 20124
Milan ☎ (02) 67581

Ireland
Piazza San Pietro in Gessate 2,
Milan ☎ (02)551 875 69

UK
Via San Paolo 7, 20121 Milan
☎ (02) 723 001

USA
Via Principe Amedo 2/10,
20121 Milan ☎ (02) 290 351

Crime

There is no need to be unduly
concerned about serious crime
in the region, but it is advisable
to take sensible precautions
and be on your guard at all
times, particularly in Milan.
• Carry as little money and as
few credit cards as possible,
and leave any valuables in the
hotel safe.
• Carry wallets and purses in
secure pockets inside your
outer clothing, wear body
belts, or carry handbags across
your body or firmly under your
arm.
• Cars, particularly hire cars,
can be a target for oppor-
tunists, so never leave your car
unlocked, and hide away or,
better still, remove items of
value.

• If your passport is lost or
stolen, report it to your
Consulate or Embassy at once.

Currency see Money

Customs and Entry Regulations

There is no limit on the impor-
tation into Italy of tax-paid
goods brought into an EU
country, provided they are for
personal consumption, with
the exception of alcohol and
tobacco which have fixed limits
governing them.

Disabled Visitors

The *Michelin Red Guide Italia*
indicates which hotels have
facilities for the disabled.
  In Britain, RADAR, at 12 City
Forum, 250 City Road, London
EC1V 8AF ☎ (0171) 250 3222,
publishes fact sheets as well as
an annual guide to facilities
and accommodation overseas,
including Italy.
  Italian National Tourist
Offices should also be able to
give information about hotels,
museums, etc. with facilities
(*see* **Tourist Information
Offices**).

Driving

Remember to drive on the
right, and give way to traffic
coming from the right –
although you may notice that

some Italian drivers take no notice of this rule.

Street parking is fraught with difficulties in many towns, but there are official car parks which are secure and convenient, or you can leave the car on the outskirts of town and walk in or take a bus.

There are petrol stations on the main routes into towns and cities, and at frequent intervals along motorways. They are normally open 7 30am-noon, and 3-7pm, but opening hours vary and depend on the season. Unleaded petrol is sold. Very few petrol stations off the motorways accept credit cards.

Each section of the motorway (*autostrada*) requires payment of a toll; a card is collected when you enter the system and handed in when you leave, and a charge is made for the distance covered.

The following speed limits apply in Italy:
Cars and Motorcycles
Motorways 130kph/80mph
(over 1 100cc);
110kph/68mph
(under 1 100cc)
Country roads 90kph/56mph
Built-up areas 50kph/31mph
Campers
Motorways 100kph/62mph
Country roads 80kph/50mph
Built-up areas 50kph/31mph

Drivers should carry a full national or international driving licence, and an Italian translation of the licence unless it is a pink European licence. Also take insurance documents including a green card (no longer compulsory for EU members but strongly recommended), registration papers for the car and a nationality sticker for the rear of the car.

Headlight beams should be adjusted for right-hand drive, and a red warning triangle must be carried unless there are hazard warning lights on the car. You should also have a spare set of light bulbs. The wearing of seatbelts is compulsory. *See also* **Accidents and Breakdowns**

Electric Current
The voltage in Italy is usually 220V. Plugs and sockets are of the round, two-pinned variety and adaptors are generally required.

Embassies *see* **Consulates**

Emergencies
Ambulance or Police ☎ 113
Fire ☎ 115

Etiquette
As in most places in the world, when visiting churches and

museums visitors are expected to dress discreetly, covering upper legs and arms. Italians are a courteous people and, although less formal than many other Europeans, greet each other with good morning – *buon giorno*, or good evening – *buona sera*. This is usual when entering a shop, for example.

Guidebooks *see* **Maps**

Health

UK nationals should carry a Form E111 (forms are available from post offices in Britain), which is produced by the Department of Health and entitles the holder to free urgent treatment for accident or illness in EU countries. The treatment will have to be paid for in the first instance, but the cost can be reclaimed later. All foreign nationals are advised to take out comprehensive insurance cover, and to keep any bills, receipts and invoices to support any claim.

Lists of doctors can be obtained from hotels, chemists (*farmacia*) or police stations, and first aid and medical advice is also available at pharmacies.

First aid (*pronto soccorso*) with a doctor is also available at airports and railway stations.

Hours *see* **Opening Hours**

Information *see* **Tourist Information Offices**

Limone sul Garda, on Lake Garda, is a popular water sports centre.

Good morning / Buon giorno
Good afternoon/evening / Buona sera
Yes/no / Si/no
Please/thank you / Per favore/grazie
Do you speak English? / Parla inglese?
How much is it? / Quanto costa questo?
The bill, please / Conto, per favore
Excuse me / Mi scusi
I'd like a stamp / Desidero un francobollo
Do you accept travellers' cheques? / Accetta travellers'
   cheques?
I don't understand / Non capisco

Language

Any effort to speak Italian will be much appreciated everywhere, and even a few simple words and expressions are often warmly received. Above are a few words and phrases to help you make the most of your stay.

Maps

A full range of maps and guides is published by Michelin. The Michelin sheet map **988** Italy (1/1 000 000) covers the whole of the country. If you are planning to tour the area, maps **428** and **429** (1/4 000 000) will help you plan your route. The *Michelin Green Guide Italy* includes information on the towns in the region, with detailed descriptions of the principal monuments, museums and other attractions, together with town maps. Information on restaurants and accommodation can be found in the *Michelin Red Guide Italia*, which is updated every year.

Medical Care *see* **Health**

Money

The monetary unit of Italy is the Italian lira, and notes are issued in denominations of 1 000, 2 000, 5 000, 10 000, 20 000, 50 000 and 100 000 lire. Coins are of 50, 100, 200 and 500 lire. All major credit cards (American Express, Carte Bleue, Visa/Barclaycard, Mastercard/Access, Diners Club and Eurocard), travellers' cheques and Eurocheques are accepted in most shops, restaurants, hotels, and some large motorway petrol stations.

There are no restrictions on the amount of currency visitors can take into Italy – perhaps the safest way to carry large amounts of money is in travellers' cheques which are widely accepted. Bureaux de change are found at airports and larger railway stations, and at banks (*see also* **Banks**).

Exchange rates vary, so it pays to shop around. You are advised not to pay hotel bills in foreign currency or with travellers' cheques since the hotel's exchange rate is likely to be higher than that of the bureaux de change.

Newspapers

Foreign newspapers and magazines can be bought all over the region in resort areas and towns, from newsagents and kiosks. Milan's newspaper is the *Corriere della Sera*.

Opening Hours

Shops are open 8.30/9am-1pm, and 3.30/4pm-7.30/8pm. In Milan, opening hours are longer.
Chemists are generally open 9am-7.30pm, Monday to Saturday, with some variations. Lists of chemists which are open late or on Sundays are displayed in every pharmacy.
Museums and galleries are usually closed on Sunday afternoon and all day Monday. They are usually open 9am-1/2pm, and sometimes from 5-8pm.
Churches The main churches are open all day but others close in the afternoons from 1pm-3pm; many stay closed after 3pm.

Photography

Good-quality film and camera equipment are readily available, but expensive, in Italy. Before taking photographs in museums and art galleries you should check with staff as photography is sometimes restricted. Generally it is permitted in

Sculpture detail, Certosa di Pavia.

state-owned museums, although the use of flash and tripods is not, but you need special permission to film in municipal museums.

Police

The *carabinieri* deal with serious crime; the *polizia* handle general crime, including lost passports and theft reports for insurance claims; the *polizia stradale* handle traffic control outside towns; and the *vigili urbani* deal with town traffic and administration. Police stations (*questura*) can be found in the main towns.

Post Offices

The main post office in Milan provides a 24-hour international telephone service, fax and telex, as well as poste restante facilities. Those collecting poste restante mail should bring their passport with them.

Otherwise, post offices are usually open from 8am-1/1.30pm, Monday to Friday, 9-noon on Saturday; main post offices in larger towns remain open all day, sometimes until 7pm.

Stamps (*francobolli*) are sold in post offices and tobacconists which display a blue sign with a white 'T'.

Public Holidays

New Year's Day: 1 January
Epiphany: 6 January
Easter Day and Easter Monday
Liberation Day: 25 April
Labour Day: 1 May
Assumption Day: 15 August
All Saints' Day: 1 November
Immaculate Conception:
    8 December
Christmas Day: 25 December
Boxing Day: 26 December

Public Transport *see* Transport

Religion

Italy is a Roman Catholic country and mass is celebrated in Italian in most churches every Sunday. For details of services in other languages, or of churches of other denominations, ask at the local tourist board or your hotel.

Smoking

Smoking is banned in churches, museums and art galleries, and is discouraged in restaurants. There are separate non-smoking compartments in trains.

Tobacconists (*tabacchi*) sell the major international brands of cigarettes, which are also on sale in some bars and restaurants.

Stamps *see* Post Offices

Taxis see **Transport**

Telephones

Italy is very well served with public telephones – on the streets, at railway stations and newsagents, and in cafés and bars. Kiosks take telephone cards (*schede telefoniche*) to the value of 5 000, 10 000 and 15 000 lire, sold at newsagents and tobacconists, or 100, 200 and 500 lire coins, or tokens (*gettoni*). You can dial anywhere in Italy and abroad from these telephone boxes.

As in most countries, telephone calls made from hotels may be more straight-forward and convenient, but they are more expensive.

Cheap rates apply between 10pm-8am, Monday to Saturday, and all day Sunday. For information, ☎ 184. Country codes are as follows:
Australia: ☎ 00 61
Canada: ☎ 00 1
Ireland: ☎ 00 353
New Zealand: ☎ 00 64
UK: ☎ 00 44
USA: ☎ 00 1
To call Italy from abroad, ☎ 00 39

Time Difference

Italian standard time is one hour ahead of GMT. Italian

Gardone's attractive waterfront, Lake Garda.

Summer Time (IST) begins on the last weekend in March when the clocks go forward an hour (the same day as British Summer Time), and ends on the last weekend in September when the clocks go back (one month before BST ends).

Tipping

A service charge of 10 or 15 per cent is usually included in the bill at hotels and restaurants in Italy, but a tip (minimum amount 1 000 lire)

is also given where the service has been particularly pleasing.

Usherettes who show you to your seat in a cinema or theatre should receive a tip, as should hotel, airport and railway porters, and lavatory attendants. Taxi drivers will expect about 10 per cent.

Tourist Information Offices

The Italian State Tourist Office (ENIT) is a good initial source of information about the region you are visiting,

Colourful balconies, Pallanza, Lake Maggiore.

including accommodation, travel and places of interest.

It has offices in the following English-speaking countries:

Australia and **New Zealand**
ENIT, c/o Alitalia, Orient Overseas Building, Suite 202, 32 Bridge Street, Sydney, NSW 2000 ☎ 2 92 471 308

Canada 1 Place Ville-Marie, Suite 1914, Montreal, Quebec, H3B 3M9 ☎ (514) 866 7667

UK 1 Princes Street, London W1R 8AY ☎ (0171) 408 1254

USA 630 Fifth Avenue, Suite 1565, New York, NY 10111 ☎ (212) 245 4822

Italy is divided into 20 regions, each with a Regional Tourist Board. The regions are further divided into provinces which each have a provincial capital, e.g. Milan, Bergamo, Trento and Verona. The provincial capitals in turn have a tourist board, called Ente Provinciale Turismo (EPT) or Azienda Promozione Turistica (APT) in Italian. These tourist boards run information offices (where foreign languages, including English, are spoken) throughout their province, which publish numerous brochures and leaflets and provide information about all aspects of the area. The bulk of the area covered by this book falls into the regions of Lombardy and Trentino, but also spills over into Veneto and Piedmont.

Tours

Tour operators offer innumerable holidays in the Lakes region, including a number of special-interest packages such as tours of gardens or villas; painting holidays are another possibility. Most of the major hotels offer coach tours to highlights of the area.

Transport

If you intend to stay at more than one place or want to explore the best of the region, a car is more or less essential. It will enable you to reach the more remote mountain valleys,

Craftsman at work in Bergamo.

particularly in the Trentino. *See* **Car Hire**. There is, however, a fairly extensive and efficient public transport network connecting the main towns and resort areas, especially around the major southern lakes.

Train: Italy's national railway (FS) is efficient and relatively inexpensive. Tickets can be purchased at stations and at many travel agents. Categories of trains are as follows: *locale* (very slow, stops often); *diretto* (fewer stops); *expresso* (stops at main towns only); Intercity trains (connects big cities only); and Eurocity trains (links major European cities). Various passes and discounts are available which can be arranged in advance at a CIT office (travel agents). East-west travel is simple, with frequent trains between Milan and Verona via Brescia, Desenzano and Peschiera. There is also direct rail access from Milan to Como, Lugano and Maggiore.

Bus: There is a good network of bus and coach routes in the region. Departure is usually from the train station if there is one. Passengers on urban buses must obtain tickets beforehand, usually from cafés and tobacconists, and 'validate' them on the bus by inserting them into a machine which stamps a time and date on them. Unlimited travel is permitted for a limited period, usually an hour. Passengers caught without a ticket or with an unvalidated one are subjected to an immediate and heavy fine. Brescia and Verona are centres for excellent country bus services.

Boat: Numerous boat trips and services are available on lakes Como, Garda, Iseo and Maggiore; at Lake Garda, it is possible to hire boats. Night cruises are also possible. Tourist offices can provide timetables (services tend to be seasonal).

Taxis: These can generally be found in special taxi ranks at railway stations and main squares of towns, and they can also be called by telephone. Fares are displayed on the meters, and there are extra charges at night, on Sundays and public holidays, for luggage and for journeys outside the town, e.g. to airports.

Vaccinations
see **Before You Go** p.112

Youth Hostels
see **Accommodation**

INDEX

Abbazia di Chiaravalle
    (Chiaravalle Abbey) 34
Angera 58-59
    Rocca Borromeo 58-59
    Museo della Bambola (Doll
      Museum) 59
Argegno 68-69
Arona 59
    San Carlone statue 59
artists, Lombardy's 20-21

Bardolino 78-79
    castle 79
    Museo del Vino 79
    San Severo 78-79
    San Zeno 78
Bassano del Grappa 106
Baveno 55
Bellagio 71-72
    Villa Melzi 72
    Villa Serbelloni 72
Bellano 70
Belvedere di Lanzo 69
Bergamo 37-41, 125
    Academia Carrara
      (Carrara Academy) 38
    Battistero (Baptistery) 40
    Cappella Colleoni
      (Colleoni Chapel) 39-40
    Città Alta (Upper Town)
      38-39
    Città Bassa (Lower Town)
      38
    Duomo (Cathedral) 40
    Palazzo della Ragione
      (Palace of Justice) 41
    Piazza del Duomo 39
    Piazza Matteotti 38
    Piazza Vecchia 39, 41
    Rocca (Fortress) 41
    Santa Maria Maggiore 39
    Teatro Donizetti 38
Bissone 64
Brescia 37, 41-43
    Broletto 42
    Castello 42
    Civico Museo Romano
      (Museum of Roman
      Antiquities) 42
    Duomo Nuovo (New
      Cathedral) 41-42
    Duomo Vecchio (Old
      Cathedral) 41-42
    Loggia 42-43
      Clock Tower 43
    Luigi Marzoli Museum 42
    Monastero di San Salvatore

e Santa Giulia 43
    Basilica of San Salvatore
      43
    Church of Santa Giulia
      43
    Museum of the
      Risorgimento 42
    Pinacoteca Tosio-
      Martinengo (Tosio
      Martinengo Art Gallery)
      43
    Tempio Capitolino (Capi-
      toline Temple) 9, 42
    Via dei Musei 42

Cadenabbia 69
Campione d'Italia 60, 63
    Madonna dei Ghirli 63
    Oratory of San Pietro 63
Cannobio 56
    Santuario della Madonna
      della Pietà 56
Cernobbio 68
    Villa d'Este 68, 84
Como 65-66
    Basilica di San Fedele 68
    Broletto 66
    Duomo (Cathedral) 67
    Museo Civico (Civic
      Museum) 67
    Palazzo Giovio 68
    Palazzo Olginati 68
    Piazza Cavour 66
    Piazza San Fedele 68
    Tempio Voltiano (Voltaic
      Temple) 68
    Villa dell'Olmo 84

Desenzano del Garda 75
    Villa Romana 75
Dongo 69-70

Garda 78
    Rocca Vecchio 78
Gardaland 111, 115
Gardone 75, 123
Ghibellines 11
Gravedona 69-70
    Palazzo Gallio
    Santa Maria del Tiglio 70
Grigna mountains 70
Guelphs 11

Intra 55
Iseo 81-82
Isola Bella 22, 23, 54
    Borromeo Palace 84
Isola Comacina 72
Isola dei Pescatori 22, 55
Isola Madre 22, 54-55

Isole Borromee (Borromean
    Islands) 22, 53-55
Isolina Virginia 83
    Museum of the Villa Onti
      83

lakes
    Caldonazzo 89
    Comabbio 83
    Como 5, 6, 64-72
    Garda 72-81
    Idro 81
    Iseo 81-82
    Lecco 64
    Ledro 8, 80-81
    Levico 89
    Lugano 59-64
    Maggiore 22, 23, 52-59
    Molveno 89-90
    Monate 83
    of Trento 89-91
    Orta 82-83
    Toblino 90
    Tovel 90, 91
    Varesa 83
Laveno-Mombello 58
Lavenone 81
Lazise 79
    castle 79
Lecco 70-71
    Ponte Azzone Visconti 71
Limone sul Garda 76, 119
Locarno 56-57
    Cimetta Cardada 57
    Madonna del Sasso 57
Lombards 10
Lugano 60-62
    Cathedral of San Lorenzo
      61
    Parco Civico (Civic park)
      61-62
    Piazza della Riforma 61
    Riva 61
    Santa Maria degli Angioli
      60
    Villa Ciani 61, 85
    Villa Favorita 62
Luino 57

Maestri Comacini 19, 65
Malcesine 78
    castle 78
Mandello 70
    San Lorenzo 70
Melide 64
Menaggio 5, 69
Milan 24-34, 106
    Arco della Pace 29
    Castello Sforzesco (Sforza
      Castle) 21, 28-29

INDEX

City Aquarium 29
Civiche Collezioni d'Arte (Municipal Art Collections) 28
Duomo (Cathedral) 22, 27-28
Galleria Vittorio Emanuele 33-34
Museo Bagatti Valsecchi 32
Museo del Duomo 28
Museo Nazionale della Scienza e Tecnica Leonardo da Vinci (Leonardo da Vinci National Museum of Science and Technology) 31
Museo Poldi-Pezzoli 31
Museum of Musical Instruments 28-29
Palazzo Reale (Royal Palace) 28
Parco Sempione 29
Pinacoteca di Brera (Brera Picture Gallery) 30
Sant'Ambrogio (Basilica of St Ambrose) 18, 32
Santa Maria della Scala 30
Santa Maria delle Grazie 32-33
Scala Museum 30
Teatro alla Scala (La Scala Theatre) 30, 108
Molveno 89, 90
San Vigilio 90
Monte Arbostora 64
Monte Baldo 78
Monte Isola 81
Monte Mottarone 23, 53
Monza 35
Duomo 35
Parco di Villa Reale 35
Morcote 63, 64
Madonna del Sasso 63, 64
Mussolini, Benito 14

Orrido di Sant'Anna 56
Orta San Giulio 82

Pallanza 55-56, 124
Villa Taranto 84
Parco del Campo dei Fiori 83
Parco Giardino Sigurtà 111
Parco Lombardo della Valle del Ticino 83
Pavia 35-37
Castello Visconteo 35
Certosa di (Charterhouse of Pavia) 22, 36-37, 121
Ponte Coperto 35

Peschiera del Garda 79
Pisogne 82
Santa Maria della Neve 82
Po
Plain 7, 9
river 7
Ponte Tresa (Tresa Bridge) 64
Porlezza 62
Porto Ceresio 63
Punta San Vigilio 78

Reno 57-58
Santa Caterina del Sasso 57-58
Riva del Garda 76-77
Palazzo Pretorio 76-77
Rocca 76
Torre Apponale (Apponale Tower) 76
Romans 9-10, 18, 25, 41, 42, 44, 49-50, 79, 80, 86-87

Sacro Monte 82-83
Sala Comacina 72
Salita Serbelloni 112
Salò 75
Cathedral 75
Palazzo Fantoni 75
San Giulio 82
Sarnico 81
Sasso del Ferro 58
Scaliger 45-46, 48, 50-51, 73, 78, 79
shopping 106-107
Sighignola 60
Sirmione 79-80
Grotte di Catullo 22-23, 80
Rocca Scaligera 80
San Pietro in Mavino 80
Santa Maria Maggiore 80
Sorico 69-70
Stresa 52-53, 103
Piazza Cadorna 53
Villa Ducale 53
Suna 55

Torbole 77-78
Dosso Casina 78
Torri di Benaco 78
castle 78
Tremezzo 69, 71
Villa Carlotta 23, 69, 84
Trentino 86-93
castles of 91-93
Pergine 91
Rovereto 92
Sabbionara d'Avio 92
Stenico 93
Thun 93
lakes of 89-91

Trento 86-88
Casa Bazzani 87
Castello del Buon Consiglio (Castle of Good Council) 87-88
Council of Trent 87
Duomo (Cathedral) 88
Museo Diocesano (Diocesan Museum) 88
Palazzo Pretorio 88
Santa Maria Maggiore 88
Torre Civica 88
Torre dell'Aquila 88

Varenna 70
Castello Vezio 70
Museo Ornitologico (Ornithological Museum) 70
Villa Monastero 70, 84
Varese 83
Basilica of San Vittore 83
Civic Museum 83
Palazzo Estense 83
Villa Mirabello 83
Verbania 55-56
Villa Taranto 56
Verona 44-51
Arche Scaligere (Scaliger Tombs) 48
Arco dei Gavi 51
Arena 22, 49-50, 108
Casa di Giulietta (Juliet's House) 48
Castel San Pietro 46, 49
Castelvecchio 50-51
Duomo (Cathedral) 46, 49
Giardini Giusti 49
Museo Archaeologico 49
Museum of Art 50
Palazzo dei Tribunali 47-48
Palazzo del Governo 48
Palazzo della Ragione 47
Piazza Bra 47, 50, 116
Piazza dei Signori 47-48
Piazza delle Erbe 47
Ponte di Pietra 46, 49
Ponte Scaligero 50-51
Santa Maria Antica 48
San Zeno Maggiore 51
Sant'Anastasia 48-49
Teatro Romano 49
Torre dei Lamberti 47
villas, lakeside 84-85
Visconti 11, 26, 27, 35
Vittoriale estate 75

weather 95-96
wines 105